Quantitative Tools of Project Management

Quantitative Tools of Project Management

David L. Olson

BEP BUSINESS EXPERT PRESS

First published in 2020 by
Business Expert Press, LLC
222 East 46th Street, New York, NY 10017
www.businessexpertpress.com

ISBN-13: 978-1-95152-783-9 (paperback)
ISBN-13: 978-1-95152-784-6 (e-book)

Business Expert Press Portfolio and Project Management Collection

Collection ISSN: 2156-8189 (print)
Collection ISSN: 2156-8200 (electronic)

Cover image licensed by Ingram Image, StockPhotoSecrets.com
Cover and interior design by S4Carlisle Publishing Services Private Ltd., Chennai, India

First edition: 2020

10 9 8 7 6 5 4 3 2 1

Table of Contents

Abstract

This book addresses the use of quantitative tools to support general project management. Part I of the book deals with critical path modeling. Part II discusses risk modeling tools to include Program Evaluation and Review Technique (PERT), critical chain modeling, and agile/scrum approaches. Project control through earned value analysis is also covered. Part III is a Microsoft Project orientation. A feature of the book is an effort to tie content to that of the Project Management Body of Knowledge (PMBOK). Each chapter includes reference to how each chapter relates to the PMBOK structure and its relationship to the 2020 Project Management Professional (PMP) Exam Outline.

Keywords

project management; estimation; quantitative models; critical path model; Project Evaluation and Review Technique; simulation; earned value

Preface

Key features include expansion of coverage of project management tools from the prior book,[1] following extraction of human and organizational material in the companion first book, Core Concepts of Project Management. This revision also focuses on general project management and on updating Project Management Institute (PMI) material. Risk management tools, including Program Evaluation and Review Technique (PERT), are reviewed, and simulation is explored to ascertain how it can better deal with project risk. Agile and SCRUM approaches are also examined, including a demonstration of critical chain project management. Earned value assessment is discussed as a means to control project implementation. The book also includes a demonstration of initial Microsoft Project application.

Note

1. D.L. Olson. 2004. *Introduction to Information Systems Project Management* (Englewood Cliffs, NJ: McGraw-Hill/Irwin, 2nd ed.).

CHAPTER 1

Estimation

Key points:
- Discussion of the estimation process through development of work breakdown structure
- Coverage of organization, scheduling, and control concepts
- Demonstration of three approaches to estimating information systems projects, with the intent of showing broad outlines of how estimation could be accomplished in other fields

---

Once a system is developed, more detailed estimation is required. At the strategic level, macro estimates were used to evaluate the project for approval. As the project moves to requirements analysis and determination of feasibility, more accurate estimates are possible as more detailed planning is conducted. During the planning process, detailed tasks (things to do—deliverables) and milestones (completed project module elements, resulting in a completed, functioning system) are identified. This chapter discusses the planning process, as well as factors important in information system project estimation. Several quantitative methods of software project estimation are explained.

The chapter demonstrates concepts using information systems project contexts, but other projects have similar features. For instance, in construction the human emphasis of information systems projects is less dominant, relying more on equipment and materials. Both contexts often rely on subcontracting in various forms. But the principles demonstrated are transferable. Two dominant estimating methods are demonstrated. In information systems, lines of code utilize some broad metric, whereas function point (FP) analysis focuses on types of activities. Regression has been used in information systems estimation, and also has been applied in construction, but care needs to be taken in both contexts to obtain accurate data.

Planning Process

Information systems projects have high levels of uncertainty. The size of the project is usually not well understood until systems analysis has been completed. Most of the unexpected delay in these projects occurs during the latter stages of testing, late in the project. Systems builders tend to report projects as on time and budget targets until the last stages of testing. But at this point, most projects are found to require additional work, often substantial in scope.

Information systems projects have several unique factors that lead to high variability in project durations, including variances in the productivity across people for specific work, and in the technology used. Resources available are often not known at the beginning of a project. Many specific resources may be planned for use on a project during the planning stages, but months later other events may arise that make it impossible to use the best people on a project.

The planning process consists of a number of steps, including the following:

- Set objectives and requirements—determining requirements
- Specify work activities—identifying specific work to be done
- Plan project organization
- Develop the schedule
- Control points—establish control mechanisms to include budgeting resources

Set Objectives and Requirements

The first step is to determine requirements. Project objectives are set in the early stages of project proposals. Once these objectives are identified, the measures of accomplishment needed to identify successful completion of the project have to be established. These are the standards for each element of the project. In building a bridge, this would be the carrying capacity of the structure. In terms of information systems projects, this would be a statement of what the final project is ultimately supposed to do.

A **statement of work**, can be viewed as a contract between the information systems development team and project end users (see Figure 1.1). The statement of work can contain product descriptions, discussion of project constraints, schedule requirements, budget limits, and an explanation of the roles and responsibilities of project participants.

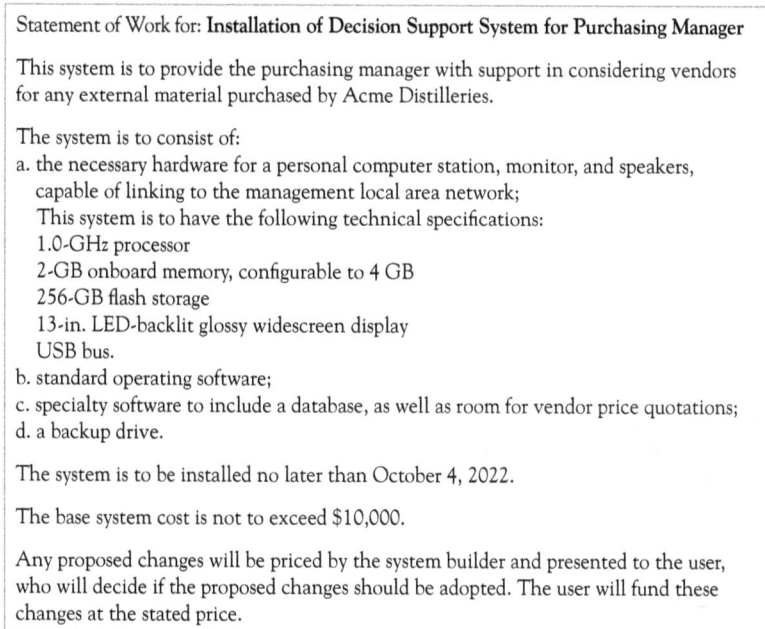

Statement of Work for: **Installation of Decision Support System for Purchasing Manager**

This system is to provide the purchasing manager with support in considering vendors for any external material purchased by Acme Distilleries.

The system is to consist of:
a. the necessary hardware for a personal computer station, monitor, and speakers, capable of linking to the management local area network;
   This system is to have the following technical specifications:
   1.0-GHz processor
   2-GB onboard memory, configurable to 4 GB
   256-GB flash storage
   13-in. LED-backlit glossy widescreen display
   USB bus.
b. standard operating software;
c. specialty software to include a database, as well as room for vendor price quotations;
d. a backup drive.

The system is to be installed no later than October 4, 2022.

The base system cost is not to exceed $10,000.

Any proposed changes will be priced by the system builder and presented to the user, who will decide if the proposed changes should be adopted. The user will fund these changes at the stated price.

Figure 1.1 Statement of work

Constraints under which the system must be developed should be identified early in the project. These include time parameters, such as deadlines. The project may have to be accomplished within existing skill levels. Levels of project complexity can be specified. Budgets are an important resource limitation. Technology might be imposed, such as using Computer-Aided Software Engineering (CASE) tools. Interoperability opportunities, such as the availability of proprietary or open systems, may be specified.

Specify Work Activities

A **work breakdown structure** is a top-down hierarchical chart of tasks and subtasks required to complete the project (see Figure 1.2). The work breakdown structure can be focused on a product, a function, or anything describing what needs to be accomplished. The work breakdown structure is hierarchical, in that different levels of detail can be described.

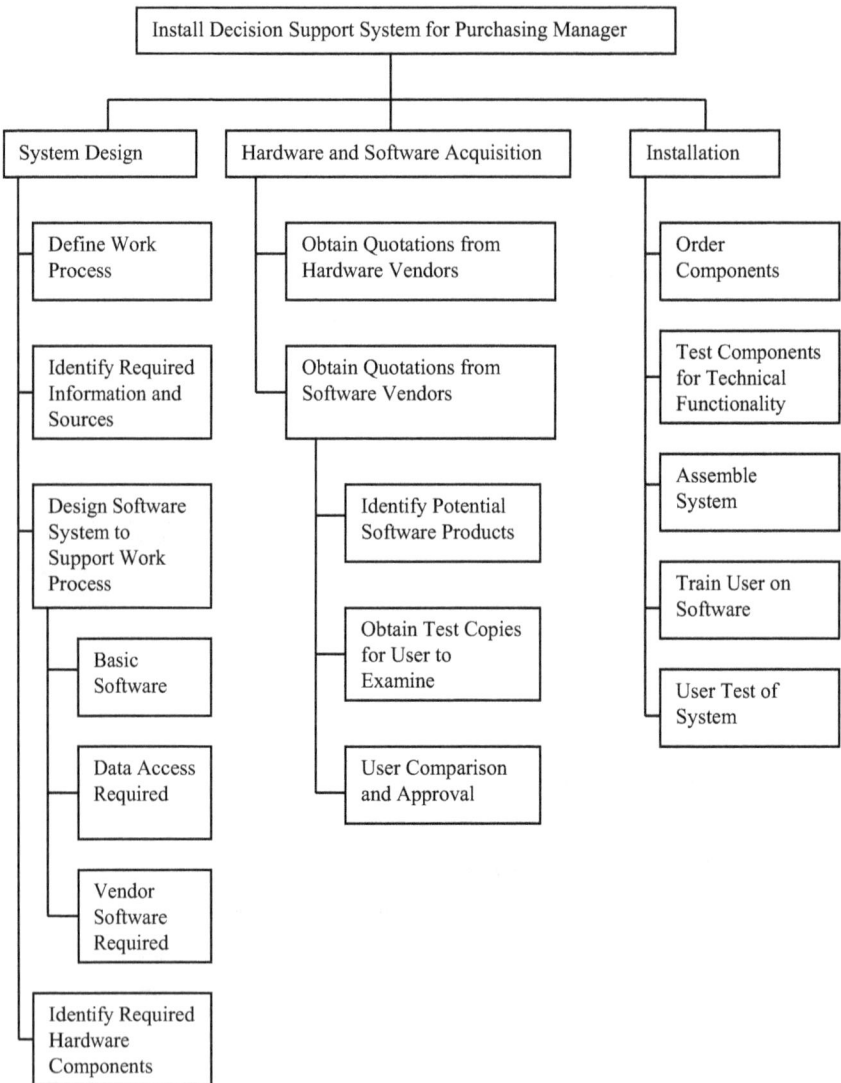

Figure 1.2 Work breakdown structure

The overall project consists of a set of major activities, or project subelements. The schedule consists of a set of tasks, usually denoting work done by a specific worker or work group. This is usually the lowest level of project activity that is used for planning. In Figure 1.2, task "System Design" is a major task with four subelements at two levels. Subactivity "Design Software System to Support Work Process" consists of three unique subactivities. Task "Installation" consists of only one level of five activities. For large projects, quite a few levels in the work breakdown structure hierarchy may be required.

A **detailed task list** is a listing of unique work packages briefly describing work to be done. The detailed task list also includes the assignment of responsibilities by job title and predecessor relationships. Predecessor relationships identify the conditions required for tasks to begin. Resources required, deliverables, and estimated durations are also provided. Figure 1.3 demonstrates a detailed task list for an example project. This information makes it possible to schedule and plan the project.

The work packages for tasks can include a summary of work to be done, predecessors (activities that must be completed before this task can be started), who is responsible, specifications for output, resources required, and deliverables. In Figure 1.3, predecessors and durations are provided for those tasks that are not subdivided. Specifications or required output could be provided as needed.

This detailed task list is the basis for estimating, scheduling, and allocating resources. The time required to accomplish each task, as well as the resources required by task, are included. Identifying these numbers is the task of **estimation** at this stage. Accurate estimation is a very difficult task. The best way to increase accuracy is to rely on experience supplemented by careful study and record keeping. It is wise to build a database of norms based on past experiences for reference in estimating future projects. Any project environment involves difficulty in estimating, because, by their nature, projects involve dealing with new activities. This is especially true in the field of information systems because of the phenomenal rate of change in technology.

There is a natural human tendency to "pad" estimates of the time required to do things. If your professor asks you how long it will take you to write a ten-page paper, would you respond with the fastest time you

Project: **Installation of Decision Support System for Purchasing Manager**

Tasks	Subtasks	Responsible Parties	Predecessors
A System Design			
A1	Define work process	system engineer, user	none
A2	Identify required information and sources	system engineer, user	A1
A3	Design software system to support work process		
	A31 Basic software	assistant	A2
	A32 Data access required	assistant, user	A2
	A33 Vendor software required	assistant, user	A2
A4	Identify required hardware components	system engineer, user	A31,A32,A33
A0	System Design Milestone		
B Hardware and Software Acquisition			
B1	Obtain quotations from hardware vendors	hardware acquisition	A0
B2	Obtain quotations from software vendors		
	B21 Identify potential software products	software acquisition	A0
	B22 Obtain test copies for user to examine	software acquisition	B21
	B23 User comparison and approval	system engineer, user	B22
B0	Hardware and Software Acquisition Milestone		
C Installation			
C1	Order components	software acquisition	B0
C2	Test components for technical functionality	assistant	C1
C3	Assemble system	assistant	C2
C4	Train user on software	trainer, user	C3
C5	User test of system	system engineer, user	C4
C0	Installation Milestone		

Task	Resources Required	Deliverable	Estimated Duration
A1	system engineer, user	document describing work process	2 days
A2	system engineer, user	list of required information sources	1 day
A31	system engineer	document describing system	3 days
A32	system engineer, user	list of data access required	1 day
A33	system engineer, user	list of software required	1 day
A4	system engineer, user	document formally identifying components	2 days
B1	hardware acquisition	list of specifications with prices	2 days
B21	software acquisition	list of software available with prices	4 days
B22	software acquisition	examination copies	10 days
B23	system engineer, user	user approval	5 days
C1	software acquisition	purchase orders	3 days
C2	system engineer	letters of certification	2 days
C3	system engineer	functioning system	1 day
C4	trainer, user	trainer certification	2 days
C5	system engineer, user	user signed approval	3 days

Figure 1.3 Detailed task list

have ever written such a paper? You would not even respond with the average time you have taken to write such a paper. You would most likely respond with an estimate that you felt was safe. If you ask a programmer how long it will take to write a specific piece of code, you will probably receive an estimate that the programmer expects to beat 80 or 90 percent of the time. The programmer's supervisor will in turn probably add an inflationary factor to allow for contingencies, such as having to use a slower programmer. This continues up the chain of command until the final estimate is made. Everyone, even management, realizes that the estimate is padded. Management then adjusts for this padding by *cutting* the estimate drastically. What results is a wild guess that may or may not have much relationship to reality.

A due date can become a self-fulfilling prophecy. If an activity actually takes less time than the due date, work is usually slowed until the due date becomes accurate. Due dates can thus have a negative impact on project performance.

Those doing the work need to be convinced that accurate estimates are in their best interest (the ability of the firm to accurately estimate what is required to do work so that they can submit competitive yet realistic prices for project work). The focus should rather be on the chain of critical activities and those activities that might become critical. (The critical chain consists of those activities that cannot be delayed without delaying the project completion time.) This is accomplished by close management attention to make sure adequate resources are provided to critical activities, and frequent reporting of the need to finish this critical work to those who are doing it.

It is very easy for estimators to be overly optimistic. At the beginning of a project, it is natural to assume that everything will work as planned. But because of the need to accomplish a wide variety of tasks, and their interrelationships, projects rarely proceed as scheduled. Rarely will things go faster than planned. This is because of the need to obtain approval of end users and the need for delivery of materials and other components.

Plan Project Organization

Organizing refers to identifying the roles in the project organization. A **responsibility matrix** is a way to allocate tasks to individuals by responsibility (see Figure 1.4). Such a matrix can be invaluable in complex projects, enabling management to quickly identify who is responsible for

Installation of Decision Support System for Purchasing Manager

Tasks	Subtasks	SE	HA	SA	TR	User
A	SYSTEM DESIGN					
A1	Define work process	x				x
A2	Identify required information and sources	x				x
A3	Design software system to support work process					
A31	Basic software	x				
A32	Data access required	x				x
A33	Vendor software required	x				x
A4	Identify required hardware components	x				x
A0	System Design Milestone	x				x
B	HARDWARE AND SOFTWARE ACQUISITION					
B1	Obtain quotations from hardware vendors		x			
B2	Obtain quotations from software vendors			x		
B21	Identify potential software products			x		
B22	Obtain test copies for user to examine			x		
B23	User comparison and approval	x				x
B0	Hardware and Software Acquisition Milestone	x				x
C	INSTALLATION					
C1	Order components			x		
C2	Test components for technical functionality	x				
C3	Assemble system	x				
C4	Train users on software				x	x
C5	User test of system	x				x
C0	Installation Milestone	x				x

KEY: SE   software engineer
       HA   hardware acquisition
       SA   software acquisition
       TR   trainer

Figure 1.4 Responsibility matrix

each activity. This matrix can also be used when forming the project team, enabling identification of what needs to be done for comparison with the capabilities of candidates.

An **organization chart** shows the reporting relationships of all involved in the project. Figure 1.5 shows the organization for the project we have been demonstrating. The organization chart outlines the communication network and coordination patterns required within the project as well. Within matrix organizational forms, this organization chart should show both primary and secondary reporting relationships. These can include not only those temporarily assigned from functional elements to the project, but also external relationships, such as the project owner and vendors.

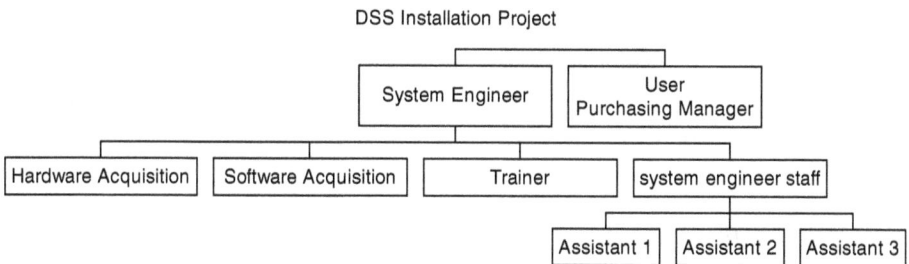

Figure 1.5 Organization chart

RACI (Responsible, Accountable, Consult, and Inform) charts are often used to clearly define roles and responsibilities. Responsible individuals own the project element. For a given activity, no more than one individual should be assigned responsibility. Accountable people are given the task of completing the activity, in support of the responsible individual. Consulting personnel are those who have the expertise needed to accomplish the project and who are available to support the responsible and accountable people. Inform people are those who need to know project status. Figure 1.6 displays a RACI chart for the project outlined in Figure 1.4.

Task	Description	SE	HA	SA	TR	User
A1	Define work process	A				R
A2	Identify required information and sources	R				C
A31	Basic software	R		C		
A32	Data access required	R		C		C
A33	Vendor software required	C	I	R	I	I
A4	Identify required hardware components	C	R			
B1	Obtain quotations from hardware vendors		R			
B21	Identify potential software products			R		
B22	Obtain test copies for user to examine			R		
B23	User comparison and approval	C		C	I	R
C1	Order components	I	I	R	I	
C2	Test components for technical functionality	R	C	C		
C3	Assemble system	R	C	C		
C4	Train users on software				R	C
C5	User test of system	C	I	I	I	R

Figure 1.6 RACI chart

Develop the Schedule

Schedules consist of the sequence of tasks from the work breakdown structure, along with their start and completion dates, and relationships to other tasks (see Figure 1.7). Schedules include not only time estimates but also resource requirements. Microsoft Project allows display of resources to the right of the bar, representing the planned activity schedule. Schedules give everyone an understandable plan and impose structure on the project and should therefore be widely distributed among members of the project team.

Schedules are the basis for resource allocation and estimated cost of monitoring and control purposes. The focus is on identifying when activities (tasks) are completed so that work can proceed on the following activities.

Control Points

Control points include milestones, checkpoint reviews, status review meetings, and staff meetings. When planning the project, control mechanisms

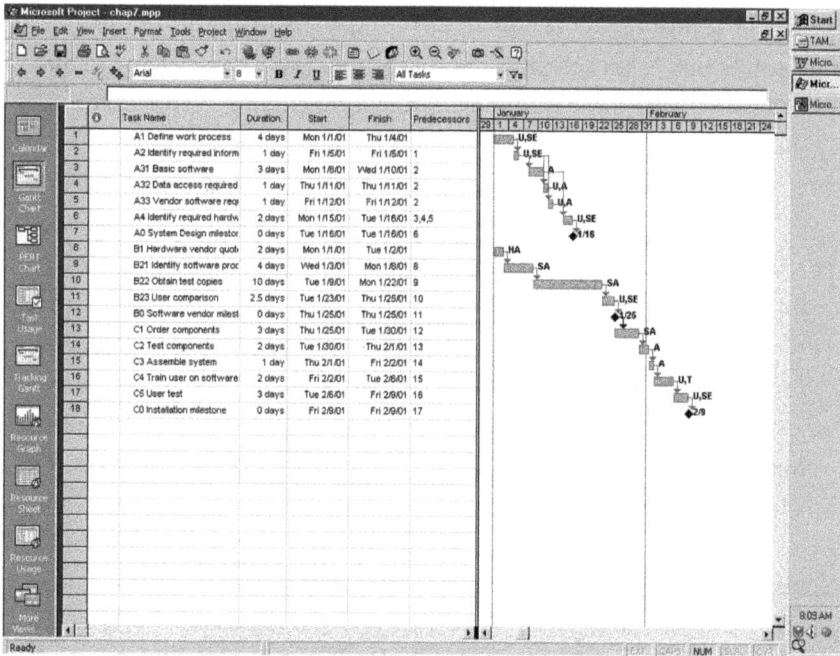

Figure 1.7 Project schedule

should also be included. Because of the existence of interrelated activities, **milestone** events are often used at the end of particular phases or group-ings of activities resulting in the completion of project subcomponents. Meetings are an important control device, providing a way to keep each element of the organization informed of what is going on. In Figure 1.7, activities 7 (System Design milestone), 12 (Software vendor milestone), and 18 (Installation milestone) are milestone activities.

There are three types of meetings that are often useful in information systems projects. **Checkpoint reviews** are held at the conclusion of each phase to determine whether or not to proceed with the rest of the project. In information system projects, this is the appropriate time to test the performance of the completed component. If its performance is less than planned, it may be necessary to change the rest of the project, and possi-bly even cancel it. **Status review meetings** are used to gather cost, quality, and schedule information. These give project management the measures needed to control the project. Finally, **staff meetings** are regularly held to maintain communication.

The primary purpose of budgets is to give management control over expenditures. A key activity is tracking actual expenditures relative to the budget. Variance reports are often used to focus on those project elements that are in the greatest amount of difficulty. When such problems are encountered, plans need to be developed to adjust to the new circumstances.

Resource usage can be measured by time period. Figure 1.8 demonstrates the schedule for the user representative before leveling, as displayed by Microsoft Project. The week beginning January 7 has a problem, with the user representative assigned to two activities at once (A32 and A33). In the plan shown in Figure 1.7, the project completion was delayed by 1 day to allow the user representative to participate in both activities. Most, if not all, project management software provides similar tools to flag when available resources are overscheduled.

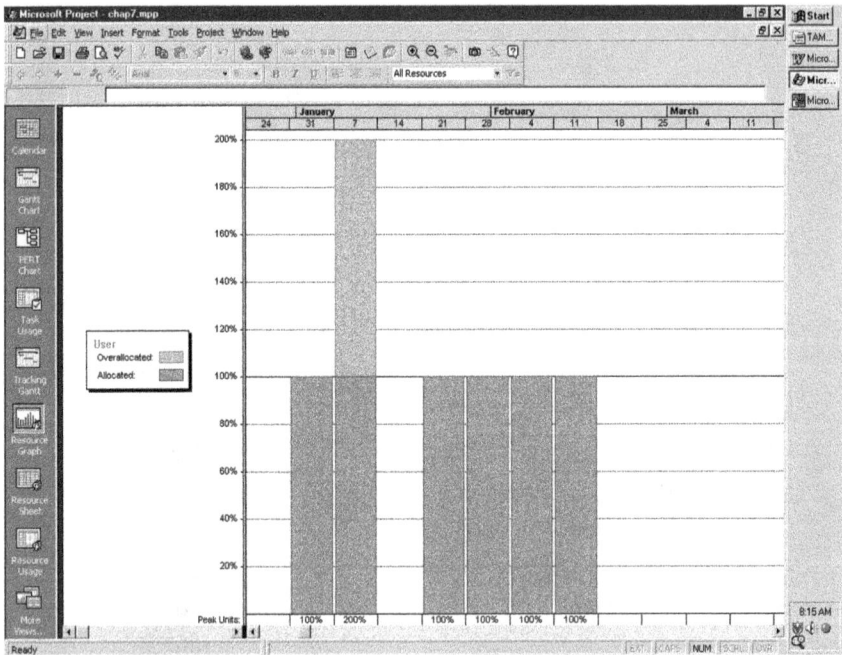

Figure 1.8 Microsoft project resource usage chart

The planning process is key to accurate cost estimation, which in turn is required for sound managerial decision making about project adoption. This is especially true for consulting organizations, which price bids to potential customers. In a competitive environment, bidding too high results in no work. Bidding too low is even worse, because it leads to undertaking projects at a loss and can ultimately lead to bankruptcy. To accurately know what the cost of delivering a project will be, you need to know the resources required. In a complex project, the duration for which these resources are needed is very difficult to estimate without a good database of the time similar activities took in the past and an analysis and understanding of special conditions that could affect these durations.

Software Estimation Methods

Estimation is a challenging activity in any project domain. Here, we demonstrate with information systems project methods, which include three broad types of estimation that appear with some similarity in other project types. These approaches are 1) to base estimates on a key metric; 2) to identify blocks of work to be accomplished and aggregate on that basis; and 3) to apply a form of regression over multiple variables. In information systems projects, the most commonly used approaches are based on source lines of code (SLOC, or LOC), type 1) estimation. The number of lines of code seems to be of less and less importance as productivity tools are developed and more productive languages are used. An example of approach 2) is to base estimation on relevant project features as in FP analysis, focusing on the functions the proposed system needs to accomplish. However, most research has not found any improvement in estimation through use of FP analysis in practice. SLOC is still widely used, and is the basis of the constructive cost model (COCOMO) system covered below, a nonlinear regression (type 3). Although these systems have noted flaws, estimating methods significantly better have not been widely reported.

In construction, similar approaches are used. Probably the most accurate is type 2), based on estimator experience. In information systems projects, the most important variable is person-hours. In construction, you need to also add equipment hours by type of equipment and materials.

The software production cycle can be described in many ways. A simple view consists of the following major elements: design and development, production, testing, installation, and maintenance. The amount of time required to develop a set of code is a function of its size. The follow-ing demonstration of the source lines of code (SLOC or LOC) and FP methods demonstrates this point.

Lines of Code

Both LOC and FP methods begin with the scientifically sound approach of gathering historical records of experiences of past projects. This histori-cal data is the basis for identifying the relationship between key measures of importance (such as the person-months of effort and dollars expended) and other factors of importance (such as the pages of documentation generated, errors encountered, system defects, and people assigned). An implementation of the LOC approach (Table 1.1) uses the following key measures per line of code.

Table 1.1 Lines of code operation

Averages of past projects		Effort	$(000)	pp. Documentation	Errors	Defects	People
LOC	20,543	33 mos.	361	1194	201	52	4
Avg per KLOC		1.606	17.573	58.122	9.784	2.531	0.195

Estimation of simple lines of code amounts to estimating how many thousand lines of code are expected and multiplying that number by each of the averages per KLOC (thousand lines of code). When a new project is encountered, an estimate is made of the lines of code that the project will require. For instance, if a new project is estimated to involve 10,000 lines of code, estimates of these measures would be as presented in Table 1.2:

Table 1.2 *Application of LOC*

Effort	1.606 × 10 thousand LOC	=	16 person-months
Budget	17.573 × "	=	$176,000
Documentation	58.122 × "	=	581 pages
Errors	9.784 × "	=	98
Defects	2.531 × "	=	25
People	0.195 × "	=	2 people

This approach is admittedly rough, but provides a very easy way to implement estimation method. Although gathering the data is time consuming, once it is obtained, it is very quick. It will be more accurate the more appropriate the data is, of course. Ideally, firms could build their database in categories by type of work, as averaging radically different projects together will lead to obvious inaccuracies. Another limitation is that it takes time to generate a database of historical project results. As with any statistical approach, the more data, the greater the confidence. However, the older the data, the less likely it is appropriate to current operations. Additionally, the model as demonstrated is totally linear, while project size may have different impacts at different size levels. More refined methods have been developed.

Function Point Analysis

Albrecht's Function Point Analysis Method supplements these project size bases of estimation. The aims of this approach are a consistent measure meaningful to the end user with rules that are easy to apply. The method can be used to estimate cost and time based on requirement specifications and is independent of the technology used.

The FP method works in a very similar way to lines of code, except that the basis for estimation is FP (reflecting, in essence, work to do). The original FP method involved counts of the number of activities in five categories (user inputs, user outputs, user inquiries, files accessed, and external interfaces). The number of functions is counted by complexity level (low, average, or high) for each factor and multiplied as in Table 1.3:

Table 1.3 Function point count calculations

Measurement parameter	Low		Average		High		Product
Number of user inputs	_____	× 3	+_____	× 4	+_____	× 6	=_____
Number of user outputs	_____	× 4	+_____	× 5	+_____	× 7	=_____
Number of user inquiries	_____	× 3	+_____	× 4	+_____	× 6	=_____
Number of files	_____	× 7	+_____	× 10	+_____	× 15	=_____
Number of external interfaces	_____	× 5	+_____	× 7	+_____	× 10	=_____

The count-total is the sum of the product column. To demonstrate on a hypothetical software proposal (see Figure 1.9) for a software project.

Demonstration of Count-Total Calculation

Software: A bank accounts record system involving:

36 user inputs	classified as simple in complexity
5 user outputs	classified as average in complexity
20 possible user inquiries	classified as simple in complexity
40 files accessed	classified as simple in complexity
3 external interfaces	classified as average in complexity

Measurement parameter	Low		Average		High		Product
Number of user inputs	_36_	× 3	+_____	× 4	+_____	× 6	=_108_
Number of user outputs	_____	× 4	+_5_	× 5	+_____	× 7	=_25_
Number of user inquiries	_20_	× 3	+_____	× 4	+_____	× 6	=_60_
Number of files	_40_	× 7	+_____	× 10	+_____	× 15	=_280_
Number of external interfaces	_____	× 5	+_3_	× 7	+_____	× 10	=_21_
TOTAL							494

Figure 1.9 Count-total calculation

The next step is to calculate F_i, which involves adding the ratings over the following 14 factors on a 0 to 5 scale, with 0 representing no impact, 1 incidental, 2 moderate, 3 average, 4 significant, and 5 essential impact. The calculation, with a hypothetical set of impacts, is shown in Table 1.4:

Table 1.4 Function point calculation

			1–5 scale
F1	Does the system require reliable backup and recovery?	Significant	4
F2	Are data communications required?	Moderate	2
F3	Are there distributed processing functions?	Significant	4
F4	Is performance critical?	Average	3
F5	Will system run in existing, heavily utilized environment?	Essential	5
F6	Does the system require online data entry?	Essential	5
F7	Does online data entry require input on multiple screens?	Incidental	1
F8	Are the master files updated online?	No influence	0
F9	Are the inputs, outputs, files, or inquiries complex?	Incidental	1
F10	Is the internal processing complex?	Incidental	1
F11	Is the code designed to be reusable?	Average	3
F12	Are conversion and installation included in the design?	Average	3
F13	Is the system designed for multiple installations across units?	No influence	0
F14	Is application designed to facilitate change and ease of use?	No influence	0
		TOTAL F	32

FPs are then calculated by the formula:

$$FP = \text{count-total} \times [0.65 + 0.01 \times \Sigma F_i]$$

In the hypothetical example, estimation of effort would be:

$$FP = 494 \times [0.65 + 0.01 \times 32] = 479.18$$

Then the estimation of required resources (Table 1.5) would be similar to that for LOC:

Table 1.5 Function point estimation

Averages of past projects	Effort	$(000)	pp. doc	Errors	Defects	People
FP=623	33 mos.	361	1194	201	52	4
Average per FP (divide by 623)	0.0530	0.5795	1.9165	0.3226	0.0835	0.0064
Multiply by new FP (479.18)	25.4	278	918	155	40	3

Although lines of code have proven useful and the FP method is also useful and widely used, estimation of software project effort continues to be a difficult task. Many other approaches continue to be generated. In part, new developments are needed because the software project environment is changing, with far less reliance on actual coding (the most predictable part of a software project).

The next model applies logarithmic regression on past data to more accurately reflect the time required to accomplish code development. COCOMO reflects the impact of learning, in that as the project progresses, programmers and developers are expected to gain in the rate of productivity.

Constructive Cost Model

Constructive cost models (COCOMO) for estimating the effort required for developing software have been promulgated. The basic COCOMO model computes software development effort on the basis of program size. An intermediate model also considers a set of cost drivers reflecting specific product, hardware, personnel, and project characteristics. The advanced model breaks out cost driver impact on each step of the software engineering process.

For relatively small, simple software projects built by small teams with good experience, COCOMO formulas for person-months of effort and development time in chronological months are:

$$\text{Person-months} = 2.4 \times \text{KLOC}^{1.05} = E \text{ for effort}$$
$$\text{Duration (months)} = 2.5 \times E^{0.38}$$

Thus, for a job of this type involving 50,000 lines of code,

$$\text{Person-months} = 2.4 \times 50^{1.05} = 145.925 \text{ months}$$
$$\text{Duration} = 2.5 \times 145.925^{0.38} = 16.6 \text{ months}$$

For software projects of intermediate size and complexity, built by teams with mixed experience and facing more rigid than average requirements, the formulas are:

$$\text{Person-months} = 3.0 \times \text{KLOC}^{1.12}$$
$$\text{Duration (months)} = 2.5 \times E^{0.35}$$

Therefore, a job of this type involving 50,000 lines of code would have the following estimates:

$$\text{Person-months} = 3.0 \times 50^{1.12} = 239.865 \text{ months}$$
$$\text{Duration} = 2.5 \times 239.865^{0.35} = 17.0 \text{ months}$$

Finally, for a software project built under rigid conditions, the formulas are:

$$\text{Person-months} = 3.6 \times \text{KLOC}^{1.2}$$
$$\text{Duration (months)} = 2.5 \times E^{0.32}$$

A job involving 50,000 lines of code under these conditions would be estimated:

$$\text{Person-months} = 3.6 \times 50^{1.2} = 393.610 \text{ months}$$
$$\text{Duration} = 2.5 \times 393.610^{0.32} = 16.9 \text{ months}$$

There are variations in COCOMO. Companies could generate their own using regression on their productivity data. There are many causes of productivity loss. For one thing, the amount of time applied by humans to actual coding is only about 20 hours per week, owing to machine downtime, emergency diversion, meetings, paperwork, sick time, and many other factors. A great deal of this waste, except for machine downtime, is recovered by using automated tools.

Interactions are activities involving coordination with others. The more interactions, the less productivity. High-level languages increase productivity by almost eliminating the programming component, but the more unpredictable activities still have to be accomplished by the project team.

Planning for Change

As we stated at the outset of the prior section, software estimation methods have been found wanting. LOC would seem to be irrelevant to contemporary system development environments, but FP analysis does not appear to be much better. As we also said at the beginning of the prior section, these methods appear to be about as good as anything at estimating software projects. Therefore, systems developers can expect high levels of change in project development duration.

Given the pace of technological business change, systems should be developed with anticipation of change. The prototyping approach, where a working version of the system is built before final design, is appropriate for some projects, where the idea is to design the product's final details *after* seeing a mock-up in action. Development principles that make sense in this environment include modularization, subroutining, documentation of interfaces, and high-level languages.

There are a number of implementations of risk analysis in software development. Buffer approaches will be discussed in Chapter 7. Another approach is to identify threats to project completion with respect to time, budget, and quality and develop contingency plans to be implemented if these threats materialize. One obvious contingency plan is to cancel the project should it encounter too many unexpected delays and budget overruns. Other contingency alternatives are to pull internal experts off other projects to get this project back on track. Outsourcing can also be used, retaining external experts from the consulting field.

Scheduling

It is a rule of thumb that coding is 90 percent complete for about half of the time it was in process. Debugging was estimated to be 99 percent complete most of the time it was underway. You have probably written a computer code and should understand this very well. Humans are optimistic. The time required for computer tasks is very difficult to estimate accurately.

In studies of government projects, where estimates were carefully updated every 2 weeks, there was very little change in estimated duration until the activity actually started. While the activity was underway, those activities that actually took less time than the estimate dropped, to reflect the new knowledge. On the other hand, when things were clearly going to take longer than estimated, the estimates were rarely changed until deep into the activity.

Milestones are concrete events denoting the completion of a project phase. When a phase of project activity (a set of related tasks, such as completion of all system design tasks in Figure 1.3) is over, including successful component testing, a milestone is completed. Milestones are scheduled as activities with zero duration, reflecting completion of a block of work.

Critical path models, to be elaborated on in Chapter 2, are network descriptions of project activities that identify activity start times and completion times. Brooks found preparation of critical path models to be their most valuable aspect. Dependencies are clearly identified, and there is value in estimating activity durations. Critical path models were meant to aid project control by allowing comparison of actual performance with planned performance. However, as a control device, model elements such as task completion status are often not updated until it is too late, at which time the system change is dramatic. When delay is first noticed, the tendency is not to report it. Project management systems provide status information giving the latest reported picture of what is going on. The key to successful management is determining when something needs to be done to correct what is going on.

Summary

Estimation of activity duration and cost is key to sound scheduling and budgeting. It is a very difficult task, because project activities are so variable in these terms.

A great deal of effort has been devoted to the accurate estimation of software development projects. Specific measures of project size include source lines of code (SLOC or LOC), the most commonly used measurement. This method is based on a concrete measure, which is attractive. But it is deficient in that it is often difficult to specify the specific lines in question. Different languages can require very different approaches for different tasks. In former times, when FORTRAN (Formula Translation) was the standard language for numerical computation and when COBOL (common business-oriented language) was the standard for data processing, estimates of lines of code were quite consistent. Now, however, with the many productivity tools available and a much greater variety of languages used, lines of code are not as useful as measures. FPs focus more on what software is intended to do. COCOMO reflects learning aspects of software productivity. These information system project estimation techniques can be applied by analogy to other project contexts.

A sound estimating procedure would identify the work to be done (the work breakdown structure), estimate the time required by resource, and estimate the money required to pay the required people or hire the required consultants or equipment. To that, time-independent items such as materials or external purchases can be added. Overhead can then be allocated following company policies.

Uncertainty is a major factor with respect to the time project activities will take. Cost is often correlated with time. Most delays are incurred in the testing phase, late in the project. It is even rarer for a project to take less time than originally estimated. This is largely due to the human factor of rechecking work if it is completed early, or sometimes stalling. Projects have on occasion been completed ahead of schedule, but not very often.

PMBOK Items Relating to Chapter 1

Initiating Process Group—processes performed to define a new project or a new phase of an existing project by obtaining authorization to start.

Planning Process Group—those processes performed to establish the total scope of the effort, define and refine the objectives, and develop the course of action required to attain those objectives.

Project Information—data and information collected, analyzed, transformed, and distributed to project team members and other stakeholders.

4.2 Develop Project Management Plan—the process of defining, preparing, and coordinating all subsidiary plans and integrating them into a comprehensive project management plan.

5.2 Collect Requirements—process of determining, documenting, and managing the stakeholder needs and requirements to meet project objectives.

5.3 Define Scope—process of documenting project features and constraints.

5.4 Create work breakdown structure (WBS)—process of subdividing project deliverables and project work into smaller, more manageable components.

6.4 Estimate Activity Resources—process of estimating the type and quantities of material, human resources, equipment, or supplies required to perform each activity.

6.5 Estimate Activity Durations—process of estimating the number of work periods needed to complete individual activities with estimated resources.

7.2 Estimate Costs—process of developing an approximation of the monetary resources needed to complete project activities.

7.3 Determine Budget—process of aggregating the estimated costs of individual activities or work packages to establish an authorized cost baseline.

Thought questions

1. Find Brooks' law, and discuss how that impacts project organization.
2. What factors make duration estimates so challenging?
3. What is the correlation between time, cost, and quality in projects?

CHAPTER 2

The Critical Path Method

Key points:
- Presentation and demonstration of the critical path method
- Description of various types of slack
- Description of resource leveling and smoothing
- Presentation of conflicts arising from multiple project scheduling
- Discussion of criticisms of the critical path method

The critical path method provides a way to easily identify the soonest a project can be completed, given that the estimated durations of activities are accurate. Even though estimated durations are usually at variance with actual outcomes, the critical path method provides a useful analysis of which activities are time bottlenecks. The input to the critical path method is a list of each activity, its expected duration, and those activities that immediately precede this activity. "Immediately precede" in this case means that predecessor activities must be completed before the subject activity can begin and that there are no other activities between the predecessor and the activity in question.

The **critical path method** provides a basis for identifying the criticality of specific activities, which can help determine which among competing activities can be delayed to stay within resource levels. A **critical activity** is an activity that must be completed on schedule or else project completion will be delayed. Therefore, critical activities are said to have no **slack**, or spare time to complete. A **critical path** is the chain of critical activities from the beginning of the project to its completion. If a project has no overall slack between the time it is to be completed and the minimum time to complete based on duration estimates, there will be at least one critical path for the project. However, there may be multiple critical paths, or more than one sequence of activities related by predecessor/follower relationships that have zero slack. To demonstrate, consider the following very simple project, consisting of five activities, as shown in Table 2.1.

Table 2.1 Demonstration activity list

Activity	Duration (weeks)	Predecessors
A Estimate cost to complete project	12	None
B Bid job and complete contract	1	A
C Build system	40	B
D Develop training	20	B
E Implement system	5	C, D

Another graphical output of the critical path method is a **Gantt chart**, which displays the early start schedule versus time (Figure 2.1). In this case, it is clear that there is only one critical path, consisting of the chain of activities A–B–C–E. Activity D has slack.

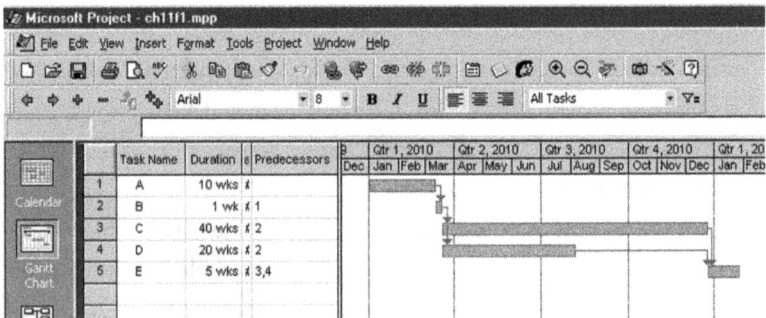

Figure 2.1 Gantt chart from Microsoft Project

This is all of the information required to develop a critical path model. The critical path algorithm is quite straightforward.

Early Start Schedule

An early start schedule (first pass) is developed (Table 2.2). For every activity that has no unscheduled predecessors, schedule the activity to start as soon as possible (either the project start time or the maximum early finish of all predecessors). The critical path schedules are optimal with respect to time. This process continues until all activities are scheduled. The early finish is the sum of the early start time plus the duration.

Table 2.2 Early start schedule

Activity	Early start	Early finish	
A Estimate cost to complete project	0	12	Releases B
B Bid job and complete contract	12	$12 + 1 = 13$	Releases C and D
C Build system	13	$13 + 40 = 53$	
D Develop training	13	$13 + 20 = 33$	With C, releases E
E Implement system	MAX(53,33)	$53 + 5 = 58$	

The project **early completion time** is the maximum early finish. In this case, the project early completion time is 58 weeks.

Networks

Quite often a **network** is displayed, which graphically displays the relationship between activities (Figure 2.2). Networks are not really needed

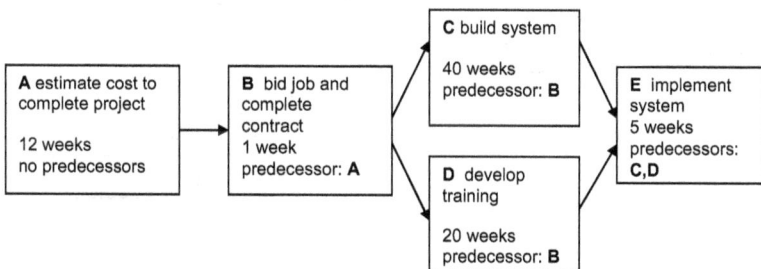

Figure 2.2 Network

for the development of early start schedules but are very useful in sorting out the relationships for late start schedules. They also provide a valuable visual aid for managers to identify relationships among activities.

Late Start Schedule

The next phase of the critical path analysis is the **late start schedule** (second pass). The late start schedule is the latest an activity can be scheduled without delaying project completion time. The final ending time for the project can be some contract deadline, which may be different from the early finish schedule, or the early finish project completion time can be used. If the deadline is earlier than the project early finish time, the project is infeasible (cannot be completed on time with given durations). If the deadline is later than the project early finish time, all activities in the project will have slack, or spare time. If the deadline coincides with the project early finish time, there will be at least one **critical path**, connecting activities in a chain with zero slack.

The late start schedule (Table 2.3) is calculated in reverse. Begin with the end time (deadline or early finish time). All activities that do not appear on the list of predecessors for unscheduled activities can be scheduled. The late finish time will be either the project end time or the minimum of the late start times for all following activities.

Table 2.3 Late start schedule

Activity	Late finish	Late start	
A Estimate cost to complete project	58	$58 - 5 = 53$	Releases C and D
B Bid job and complete contract	53	$53 - 20 = 33$	
C Build system	53	$53 - 40 = 13$	With D, releases B
D Develop training	MIN (13,33)	$13 - 1 = 12$	Releases A
E Implement system	12	$12 - 12 = 0$	

Slack

Slack (float) is the difference between the late start and early start schedules. (It doesn't matter which you use, because in both cases the difference between them is the duration.) Those activities with zero slack are critical. If they are delayed, the project completion will be delayed. There can be more than one critical path for a project, and the project network presented in Figure 2.2 can be useful in ensuring identification of each critical path. Calculations are given in Table 2.4:

Table 2.4 Slack calculations

Activity	Early start	Early finish	Late start	Late finish	Slack	
A Estimate cost to complete project	0	12	0	12	0	Critical
B Bid job and complete contract	12	13	12	13	0	Critical
C Build system	13	53	13	53	0	Critical
D Develop training	13	33	33	53	20	
E Implement system	53	58	53	58	0	Critical

Slack in the preceding case exists for only one activity, D. More complex projects will include slack for multiple activities, such as the following project (Table 2.5).

Table 2.5 Second example project

Activity	Duration (weeks)	Predecessors
A Rough design of advertising plan	1	None
B Convince project manager	3	A
C Develop marketing plan	3	B
D Identify media alternatives	2	B
E Print materials	1	C
F Brief sales force	2	B
G Select media	1	D

This project has the following slacks (Table 2.6):

Table 2.6 Display of slacks

Activity	Early start	Early finish	Late start	Late finish	Slack	
A Rough design of advertising plan	0	1	0	1	0	Critical
B Convince product manager	1	4	1	4	0	Critical
C Develop marketing plan	4	7	4	7	0	Critical
D Identify media alternatives	4	6	5	7	1	
E Print materials	7	8	7	8	0	Critical
F Brief sales force	4	6	6	8	2	
G Select media	6	7	7	8	1	

A Gantt chart for this project is shown in Figure 2.3.

		W	E	E	K	S			
Activity	Duration	1	2	3	4	5	6	7	8
A rough design of advertising plan	1 week								
B convince product manager	3 weeks								
C develop marketing plan	3 weeks								
D identify media alternatives	2 weeks							s	
E print materials	1 week								
F brief sales force	2 weeks							s	s
G select media	1 week								s
	Scheduled								
	Slack	s							
	Critical								

Figure 2.3 Gantt chart

In this case, activities D, G, and F all have one unit of slack. The Gantt chart for this project shows clearly that activity F is independent of D and G, so if a week is lost in briefing the sales force, it interferes with nothing else. This case is **independent slack** (free float). On the other hand, if identifying media alternatives should take an extra week, the slack of 1 week is shared with that of activity G, which would become critical if the slack on activity D were used up. This case is **shared slack.**

Project management software includes the ability to have a number of precedence relationships. The default is generally predecessor finish = follower start. Other options include predecessor start = follower start, or predecessor start = follower start plus some lag time.

The critical path method provides a useful means of identifying the earliest a project can be completed, as well as identifying those activities that are critical. Critical activities need to be managed more closely than slack activities. This is because if any delay is experienced on a critical activity, the project completion will be delayed. On the other hand, if things are delayed for activity D in our first example, it doesn't really matter until 20 spare days are wasted. However, one should be careful, because once all of an activity's slack is exhausted, it also becomes critical.

There is a bias in projects in that activity delays accumulate, while gains from finishing early do not. This is because when an activity is late, those that must wait for it to be completed start later than scheduled. On the other hand, if an activity should be finished before it was scheduled to finish, the advantage can rarely be used, because in complicated projects different crews and materials have to be gathered and many different people need to be coordinated. The early finish time is not usually known much ahead of the activity's completion. Therefore, it is very difficult to gather all of the following activities' resources together in time to start early.

Once the final planned time schedule is developed, it can be used to estimate costs, such as expenditures for human resources, materials, and overhead. Resource time requirements are a major component of estimated cost. Also important are materials used, as well as vendor-delivered products. Overhead expenses can be estimated independently of work volume. Obviously, since time is a major element in estimating budgets, one of the major reasons projects run over budget is that they take more time than expected.

Project managers usually focus on scheduling the critical chain of activities closely to make sure that they have the resources needed to proceed according to schedule. The critical chain of activities includes those activities that are critical (as long as managerial control can influence their duration) but is not limited to these activities. Activities with very little slack can become problems if they are delayed up to or beyond their slack. Therefore, the slack of noncritical activities should also be monitored to make sure that new critical activities are identified.

Resource Leveling

The critical path model we have considered so far has assumed unlimited resources. **Resource leveling** is the process of spreading out the early start schedule so that the maximum number of a particular resource required can be reduced. For instance, if a particular specialist is needed to accomplish more than one activity and these activities happen to be scheduled during common periods of time, something would have to give. One or the other of the activities sharing the common resource would have to be delayed (or additional resources would have to be acquired).

To demonstrate, consider a project (network in Figure 2.4) with the following data:

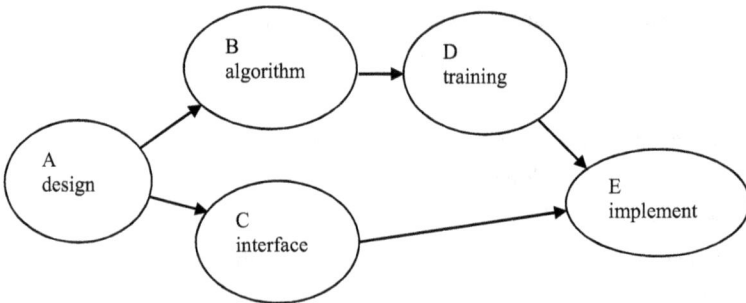

Figure 2.4 Network for leveling project

The project data is given in Table 2.7.

Table 2.7 Leveling project data

Activity	Duration (weeks)	Pred	Early start	Early finish	Late start	Late finish	Slack	Resource
A Design	3	None	0	3	0	3	0	
B Algorithm	5	A	3	8	3	8	0	Specialist
C Interface	6	A	3	9	6	12	3	Specialist
D Training	4	B	8	12	8	12	0	
E Implement	3	C,D	12	15	12	15	0	

Figure 2.5 presents the schedule for this project.

Activity	Duration	W 1	E 2	E 3	K 4	S 5	6	7	8	9	10	11	12	13	14	15
A design	3 w	■	■	■												
B algorithm	5 w				■	■	■	■	■							
C interface	6 w				▨	▨	▨	▨	▨	▨	s	s	s			
D training	4 w								■	■	■	■				
E implement	3 w													■	■	■
	Scheduled	▨														
	Slack	s														
	Critical	■														

Figure 2.5 Schedule for leveling project

If the same specialist was required for both activities B and C, they could not be accomplished concurrently. This means that the original critical path model is infeasible. Either B or C must be delayed. The decision as to what to delay is difficult to make if you are after the guaranteed best answer. For small projects, you might as well check all of the possibilities. For instance, in this case there are only two activities to delay. If B is delayed, it cannot start until week 10, when both activity A is completed and the specialist is through with activity C (Table 2.8).

Table 2.8 Leveled project after B delayed

Activity	Duration (weeks)	Pred	Start	Finish	Slack	Resource
A Design	3	None	0	3	0	
B Algorithm	5	A	9	14	0	Specialist
C Interface	6	A	3	9	0	Specialist
D Training	4	B	14	18	0	
E Implement	3	C,D	18	21	0	

Figure 2.6 gives the leveled schedule for this project. In this case, nothing is slack, because delaying any activity will delay the end of the project. We can see this, although the method of using only predecessors will not yield that result, because of the need to consider the limitation on the number of specialists.

		W	E	E	K	S															
Activity	Duration	1	2	3	4	5	6	7	8	9	10	11	12	13	14	15	16	17	18	19	20	21
A design	3 w	▓	▓	▓																		
B algorithm	5 w										x	x	x	x	x							
C interface	6 w				x	x	x	x	x	x												
D training	4 w															▓	▓	▓	▓			
E implement	3 w																			▓	▓	▓
	Specialist	x																				

Figure 2.6 Leveled project

The alternative is to delay activity C. This yields Table 2.9.

Table 2.9 Leveled project after B delayed

Activity	Duration (weeks)	Pred	Start	Finish	Slack	Resource
A Design	3	None	0	3	0	
B Algorithm	5	A	3	8	0	Specialist
C Interface	6	A	8	14	0	Specialist
D Training	4	B	8	12	2	
E Implement	3	C,D	14	17	0	

In this case, activity D will have a slack of 2. The total project is completed in 17 weeks instead of the 21 weeks obtained by delaying activity B (see Figure 2.7). This is still a significant delay, as the original critical path schedule provided for only 15 weeks.

		W	E	E	K	S												
Activity	Duration	1	2	3	4	5	6	7	8	9	10	11	12	13	14	15	16	17
A design	3 w	▓	▓	▓														
B algorithm	5 w				x	x	x	x	x									
C interface	6 w									x	x	x	x	x	x			
D training	4 w								▓	▓	▓	▓		s	s			
E implement	3 w															▓	▓	▓
	Specialist	x																

Figure 2.7 Alternative leveled project

Although there is no guaranteed best way of deciding which activity to delay when sharing scarce resources, it usually works well to use a priority system. A good choice would be to schedule critical activities first, and if more than one critical activity shares the scarce resource, a second priority that is often used is to schedule the longest activity among those selected by the first priority. If multiple resources are limited, an alternative priority could be given to scheduling the resource with the greatest number of limited resources. Project management software usually levels projects for you. They vary in what priority rules they use.

Resource Smoothing

Resource leveling focuses on extending schedules so that particular resources are not overscheduled. **Resource smoothing** focuses on adjusting schedules to obtain a level amount of work for a given resource. This includes possible extension (or compression) of activities to make work volume more even. It can also include identifying gaps in the work schedule that management might be able to fill by finding extra work.

Consider a multiple project operation in the information technology industry (Figure 2.8). Four resources are involved: crews for design, for production, for testing, and for installation of information technology products. For simplicity, assume that these four activities are accomplished in sequence in the order given. The firm currently has three projects, all with a deadline of being completed by the end of week 20.

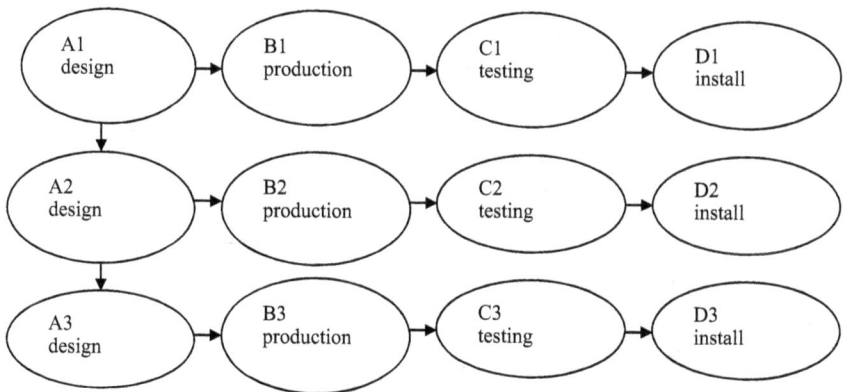

Figure 2.8 Network for smoothing projects

Project data are displayed in Table 2.10.

Table 2.10 Project inputs for smoothing

Activity	Duration (weeks)	Predecessor	Start	Finish	Resource
A1 Design	2	None	0	2	Design crew
B1 Production	4	A1	2	6	Production crew
C1 Test	2	B1	6	8	Testing crew
D1 Install	1	C1	8	9	Installation crew
A2 Design	2	A1	2	4	Design crew
B2 Production	5	A2	4	9	Production crew
C2 Test	3	B2	9	12	Testing crew
D2 Install	1	C2	12	13	Installation crew
A3 Design	4	A2	4	8	Design crew
B3 Production	6	A3	8	14	Production crew
C3 Test	3	B3	14	17	Testing crew
D3 Install	1	C3	17	18	Installation crew

The Gantt chart for this schedule is shown in Figure 2.9.

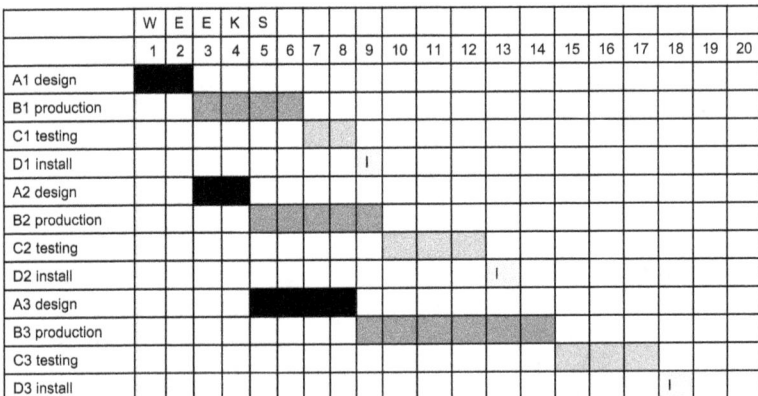

Figure 2.9 Gantt chart for multiple projects

Usages for each resource are given in Figure 2.10, with a blockout indicating the resource required by week. For instance, one design crew is required in weeks 1 through 8 and none thereafter. One production crew is needed in weeks 3 and 4, and two production crews in weeks 5 and 6.

Design	W	E	E	K	S															
	1	2	3	4	5	6	7	8	9	10	11	12	13	14	15	16	17	18	19	20
# crews needed:																				
Two																				
One	■	■	■	■	■															

Production	W	E	E	K	S															
	1	2	3	4	5	6	7	8	9	10	11	12	13	14	15	16	17	18	19	20
# crews needed:																				
Two						■			■											
One			■	■	■	■	■	■	■	■	■	■								

Testing	W	E	E	K	S															
	1	2	3	4	5	6	7	8	9	10	11	12	13	14	15	16	17	18	19	20
# crews needed:																				
Two																				
One						■			■						■					

Install	W	E	E	K	S															
	1	2	3	4	5	6	7	8	9	10	11	12	13	14	15	16	17	18	19	20
# crews needed:																				
Two																				
One								I					I					I		

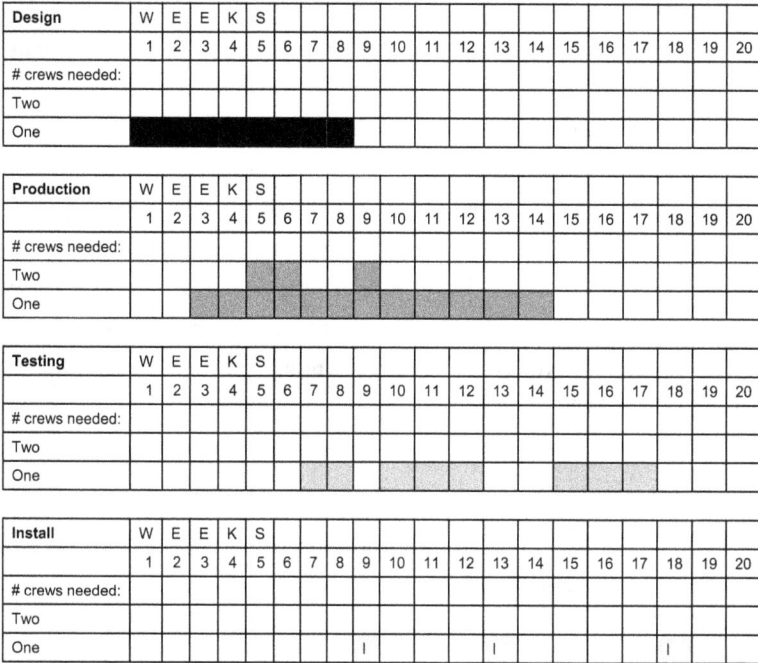

Figure 2.10 Resource usage by crew

A smooth schedule is one where a resource is working the same level of activity each time period. These resource usage charts indicate that there are two types of smoothing that might be useful: gaps in work to do, and excess work to do. When there is no work to do, a valley (no activity) is encountered. When there is too much work scheduled for a period, a peak occurs. There are valleys for the testing and installation crews. The only peaks occur for the production crew.

For all four crews, slack resources exist in that there are periods where no work is currently scheduled. This is because greater resource capacity exists than work required. Some spare resources are required to cover the inevitable uncertainty in projects. Efficiency, on the other hand, seeks to utilize all resources at their capacity at all times. Being careful to ensure that important project activities are not delayed for lack of resource, management may be able to increase efficiency by finding useful activities for resources during their unscheduled periods (or laying off crews when no work is to be done). One approach is investment in training and development activities. Another approach is to find more work. However, it is apparent here that there is also an imbalance across resources. If management were to obtain more work similar to what they have, the production crew would fall further and further behind, because their work per project is always longest. The gaps for the testing crew, and especially for the installation crew, would get wider and wider. Sound management practice here calls for balancing, through hiring additional production crews. If a great deal of similar work is obtained, more analysis crews might be called for as well. As a simple fix to this operation's problem, we add a second production crew to accomplish production work on the second project in Figure 2.11.

	W	E	E	K	S															
	1	2	3	4	5	6	7	8	9	10	11	12	13	14	15	16	17	18	19	20
A1 design	■	■																		
B1 production			1	1	1	1														
C1 testing																				
D1 install								I												
A2 design			■	■																
B2 production					2	2	2	2	2											
C2 testing																				
D2 install												I								
A3 design					■	■	■													
B3 production								1	1	1	1	1	1							
C3 testing																				
D3 install																		I		

Figure 2.11 Schedule with second production crew

The schedules for each of the production crews now are smoothed in the sense that they are not overscheduled (Figure 2.12).

Production 1	W	E	E	K	S															
	1	2	3	4	5	6	7	8	9	10	11	12	13	14	15	16	17	18	19	20
# crews needed																				
Two																				
One			1	1	1	1			1	1	1	1	1	1						

Production 2	W	E	E	K	S															
	1	2	3	4	5	6	7	8	9	10	11	12	13	14	15	16	17	18	19	20
# crews needed																				
Two																				
One					2	2	2	2	2											

Figure 2.12 Smoothed production crews

However, there is obviously more waste time that management needs to fill.

The second smoothing condition is to lower the peak workloads. This requires either delaying the schedule or hiring additional resources (demonstrated in the last section). Delaying the schedule (returning to the case using one production crew) can eliminate the excess workload (Figure 2.13).

	W	E	E	K	S															
	1	2	3	4	5	6	7	8	9	10	11	12	13	14	15	16	17	18	19	20
A1 design	■	■																		
B1 production			1	1	1	1														
C1 testing							x	x												
D1 install									x											
A2 design					■	■														
B2 production							2	2	2	2	2									
C2 testing												x	x	x						
D2 install															x					
A3 design							■	■	■											
B3 production												1	1	1	1	1	1			
C3 testing																		x	x	x
D3 install																				

Figure 2.13 Delayed (smoothed) schedule

However, eliminating the overscheduling entirely using existing resources would require extending the last project into week 21. The resource usages would now be as shown in Figure 2.14.

Smoothing is a managerial decision. The ideal would involve balancing crew capacities so that each crew could work the same amount each time period. That is what assembly line operations do. That requires a highly predictable environment, which simply does not exist in projects. Projects will inevitably experience gaps in work, along with some periods of critical resource shortage. The quality of project management can be measured on a scale of efficiency by the proportion of waste time encountered. However, priority should be given to ensuring that critical activities have the resources they need, even if it involves some waste. It is more important to get the job done right, on time, and within budget, than to obtain a perfectly smooth schedule.

Design	W	E	E	K	S															
	1	2	3	4	5	6	7	8	9	10	11	12	13	14	15	16	17	18	19	20
# crews needed:																				
Two																				
One	████	████	████	████																

Production	W	E	E	K	S															
	1	2	3	4	5	6	7	8	9	10	11	12	13	14	15	16	17	18	19	20
# crews needed:																				
Two																				
One		▓	▓	▓	▓	▓	▓	▓	▓	▓	▓	▓	▓	▓	▓	▓				

Testing	W	E	E	K	S															
	1	2	3	4	5	6	7	8	9	10	11	12	13	14	15	16	17	18	19	20
# crews needed:																				
Two																				
One					▓	▓				▓	▓		▓					▓	▓	

Install	W	E	E	K	S																
	1	2	3	4	5	6	7	8	9	10	11	12	13	14	15	16	17	18	19	20	21
# crews needed:																					
Two																					
One								I						I							I

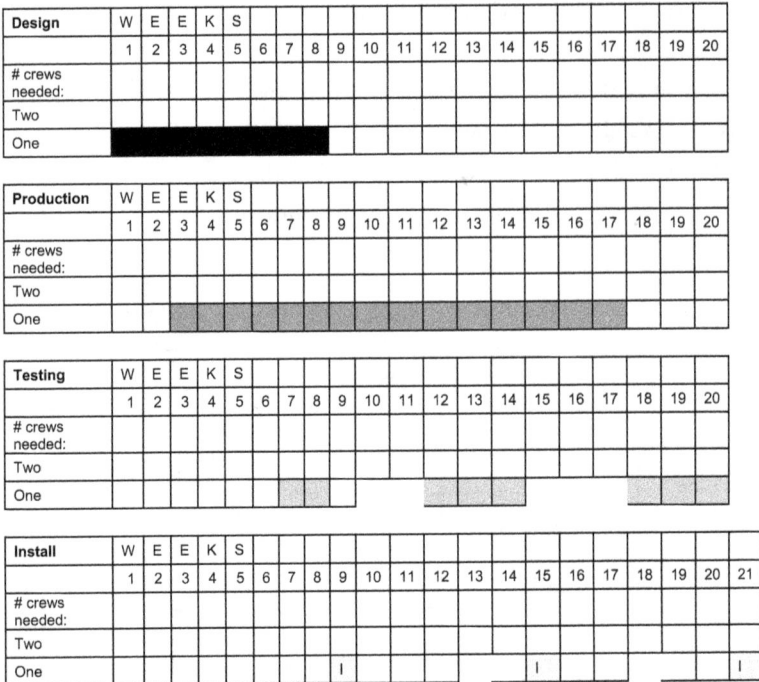

Figure 2.14 Smoothed schedule by crews

Multiproject Environments

Many organizations have evolved into organizations that manage projects as the focus of their business. This has long been true in the construction industry, where firms develop skill and equipment expertise that can be applied to a type of work, giving them competitive advantage. It has also long been true in the accounting field, where large firms develop a pool of experts in various fields that can be utilized on the problems of many firms. Information system project management has evolved from the accounting field, with many firms offering expertise that is available for hire. This is probably the most common form of outsourcing, applying expertise from consulting firms for specific problems within organizations. The matrix form of organization is especially appropriate in this environment, with pools of experts trained to a high state of development in their specialty, available on call to cope with work as it is acquired.

Both in information systems and in other fields such as construction, the vast majority of projects occur in a multiple project environment.

Projects in this environment tend to be smaller than projects found in other environments. The reason for dealing with multiple projects is to share key resources, which would otherwise be underutilized. Critical resources of this type would be the bottlenecks that make sense to use as the top priority in scheduling. The scheduling of projects subject to resource smoothing was discussed earlier. In addition to the complications involved in scheduling critical resources, there are additional sources of change in multiple project environments. As new projects are obtained, and old projects encounter difficulties, the priority for use of critical resources is liable to change. For instance, a key production crew might have originally been scheduled to work on a project for the first 3 weeks in March. After one of these weeks' work was completed, an emergency requirement might arise where this crew could help. Top management has the decision of disrupting this current project to fix problems on the project with the emergency. It often makes economic sense to have one project suffer for the greater good of the firm overall. Management is responsible for setting priorities and determining which projects will receive top priority.

To demonstrate the problems involved in multiple project management, assume a consulting firm does work requiring three crews (design crew, production crew, and training crew). To simplify matters, assume the firm does projects involving three activities, performed in sequence. Therefore, for each project, the design crew performs its work, which must be completed before the production crew can start its work, which in turn must be completed before the training crew does its work. Currently, the firm has three projects in progress, as shown in Table 2.11.

Table 2.11 Project data

Project	Design	Production	Training	Deadline
A	4 weeks (completed)	7 weeks	3 weeks	Week 20
B	3 weeks	5 weeks	1 week	Week 10
C	1 week	4 weeks	1 week	Week 10

The current schedule selected by management (showing only 30 weeks) is shown in Figure 2.15.

	W	E	E	K																										
	1	2	3	4	5	6	7	8	9	10	11	12	13	14	15	16	17	18	19	20	21	22	23	24	25	26	27	28	29	30
Design	C	B	B	B	A	A	A	A																						
Production	C	C	C	C	C	B	B	B	B	B	A	A	A	A	A	A	A													
Training						C					B							A	A	A										

Figure 2.15 Initial schedule

After the second week, the firm has completed its work as planned and obtained two new jobs, as shown in Table 2.12.

Table 2.12 Added projects

Project	Design	Production	Training	Deadline
D	5 weeks	9 weeks	3 weeks	Week 30
E	4 weeks	6 weeks	3 weeks	Week 20

This yields the following updated schedule (Figure 2.16):

This plan is infeasible within available resources. At the added cost of training new crews, some of this could be alleviated, but not necessarily at lowest cost. The point overall is that multiple project environments have high levels of uncertainty, as new jobs are acquired (and possibly canceled) that make optimized and densely packed resource schedules highly unrealistic. Here, we only hypothesized minor duration extension, whereas in reality delays of much greater consequence can occur. Added complications of redirecting experienced crews to priority projects in the middle of work tasks can create additional chaos. Overall, operation in a multiple project environment is an extremely interesting endeavor.

Critical Path Criticisms

As with any model, the critical path approach makes a number of assumptions. Usually, the more convenient the assumptions are for mathematical solution, the less realistic the assumptions are relative to the real decision. The critical path model as demonstrated earlier is very useful in identifying the soonest one can expect to complete a project. But we have seen in previous chapters that things rarely proceed as planned and that in practice the original critical path plan usually requires significant modification as the project proceeds and more accurate activity durations are obtained. There is usually significant variance in possible durations of activities, with options available to speed selected activities. Crashing provides one means of obtaining greater understanding for these situations. One approach to uncertainty is to focus on scheduling milestones. Uncertainty in activity durations is addressed by Program Evaluation

	W	E	E	K																										
	1	2	3	4	5	6	7	8	9	10	11	12	13	14	15	16	17	18	19	20	21	22	23	24	25	26	27	28	29	30
Design	**C**	***B***	B	B	A	A	A	A	E	E	E	E	D	D	D	D	D	E	E	E	E	E	E	E	D	D	D	D	D	D
Production	C	C	C	C	C	B	B	B	B	B	A	A	A	A	A	A	A	A	A	A	E	E	E	E	E	E	D	D	D	D
Training						C					B							A	A	A			E	E	E	E				

Figure 2.16 Updated schedule

and Review Technique (PERT) models and simulation, but those get involved. Another key idea is that the critical path includes those activities that should be most closely managed. Critical activities are those that need close monitoring. But those activities with apparent slack can become critical and should not be ignored.

The critical path model assumes unlimited resources. We have discussed leveling as a means of analyzing the effects of limited resources. An additional extension of this concept is smoothing. Projects typically involve highly variable workloads, with employment starting at a very low volume, jumping to high levels in the middle of the project, and then in general declining. This overall trend masks even greater variations for the workload of specific skill sets, which can be highly erratic. Smoothing seeks to level the workload of the project, sacrificing minimum time for a more even workload. In information system projects, this is less important, as the usual condition is many projects going on at once, with more than enough work for individuals on other projects as soon as their work on this project is completed. The matrix form of organization, discussed in Chapter 3, is highly appropriate for this environment, allowing individuals to be shuffled into a particular project to perform their specialty and then moved on to the next project requiring their services.

The critical path model assumes that activities can be addressed as entities, with clear beginning and ending points. In reality, the content of complex projects changes over time. As new events unfold, project progress may require change in direction. An obvious impact relative to information systems projects is the outcome of testing. According to plan, testing will find that everything was successfully built as scheduled. In reality, the outcome of testing is highly uncertain. There is a possibility that testing will find that the system components do perform as designed. If they don't, however, new activities will be required: to identify the cause of the problem, to decide how to revise the system, and quite possibly to build new system components.

Summary

The critical path method provides project managers with valuable information. The criticality of project activities can be identified, and those activities that are critical can be managed more closely. The critical path method provides an estimate of how long the project will take if everything takes no longer than estimated. The critical path method displays what can happen owing to predecessor relationships. Crashing provides a means of comparing the trade-off in cost and time in project scheduling. However, the critical path method assumes unlimited resources, which may not be realistic.

There are some things managers can do when facing resource limits. Buffers provide a way to better manage the chain of critical activities. Most project management software systems allow managers to level resources, generally following a priority system as we have outlined. While not guaranteed to provide the best solution, this ability of software packages to level resources is extremely useful.

Projects can also be leveled to stay within available resources and even smoothed to more efficiently schedule resources. Project management software is very good at accomplishing the task of leveling project activities to stay within prescribed resource levels. The solutions provided are not necessarily the best possible but are usually very good. The activity of smoothing is not as critical in project management, because efficiency is not as important as dealing with the high levels of uncertainty present in projects. Smoothing in uncertain environments is usually not effective.

The problems of managing multiple projects arise in most large organizations. The biggest difference in one large project versus many smaller projects is that in the large project, the project team is able to focus on attaining one set of objectives. In a multiple project environment, scarce resources need to be shared by many competing projects, and hard decisions have to be made to further overall organizational goals rather than focusing on the goals of specific projects.

PMBOK Items Relating to Chapter 2

6.1 Plan Schedule Management—process of establishing the policies, procedures, and documentation for planning, developing, managing, executing, and controlling the project schedule.

6.2 Define Activities—process of identifying and documenting the specific actions to be performed to produce the project deliverables.

6.3 Sequence Activities—process of identifying and documenting relationships among the project activities.

6.5 Develop Schedule—process of analyzing activity sequences, durations, resource requirements, and schedule constraints to create the project schedule model.

9.2 Estimate Activity Resources—develop estimates of needed resources to accomplish the project.

Thought questions

1. A network is not required to calculate start and finish times. What value does it provide?

2. What is the value of focusing managerial efforts on the critical path (or paths)? Does this create any related dangers?

3. What is a milestone, and what value does it provide?

CHAPTER 3

Project Crashing

Key point:
- Application of logic to consider alternative ways to accomplish a task at different costs

---

Another possibility is that extra resources can be acquired to complete critical activities quicker. This creates a problem for management, trading off quicker completion time with higher cost. If the savings from faster completion time are known, then the problem is simply one of minimizing cost. Often, however, it is a matter of risk in that you know some activities are subject to delay, and earlier planned finishing times are far safer than those plans that push things to some deadline.

To demonstrate crashing, consider a problem of importing some critical piece of equipment from Australia, which you have contracted to install for a client. Figure 3.1 gives a network for this project. You have agreed to get the equipment installed and running in 12 days. If you are late, you will pay a penalty of $500 per day for each day beyond the contracted 12 days.

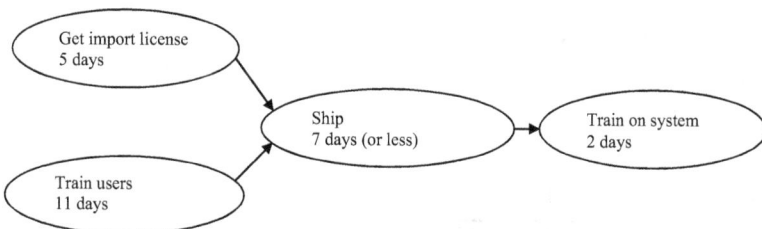

Figure 3.1 Network for delivery from Australia

The critical path calculations for the basic model are shown in Table 3.1.

Table 3.1 Slack calculations

Activity	Duration (days)	Pred	Early start	Early finish	Late start	Late finish	Slack
A Get import license	5	None	0	5	0	5	0
B Ship	7	A	5	12	5	12	0
C Train Users	11	None	0	11	1	12	1
D Train on System	2	B,C	12	14	12	14	0

Figure 3.2 displays the schedule for the base case.

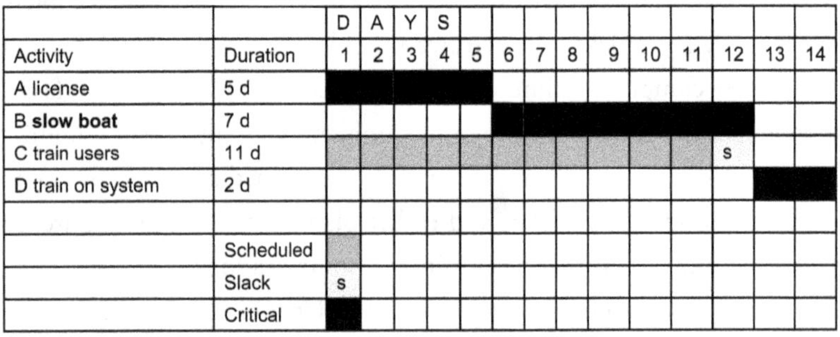

Activity	Duration	D	A	Y	S	5	6	7	8	9	10	11	12	13	14
		1	2	3	4	5	6	7	8	9	10	11	12	13	14
A license	5 d	■	■	■	■	■									
B slow boat	7 d						■	■	■	■	■	■	■		
C train users	11 d	�											s		
D train on system	2 d													■	■
	Scheduled	▒													
	Slack	s													
	Critical	■													

Figure 3.2 Australian delivery schedule

The critical path, which takes 14 days, is A–B–D. Activity C has 1 day of slack. But this plan involves a penalty of $1,000, because it is two days late. The options available for activity B ship are shown in Table 3.2:

Table 3.2 Logistics options

Option	Time (Days)	Cost ($)	
Slow boat	7	100	The base option
Fast boat	6	300	
Bush airplane	5	400	
N airplane	3	500	
Chartered plane	1	900	

The base plan uses the least cost method, the slow boat. However, it incurs penalties of $1,000. Clearly it would be cost effective to adopt a faster delivery method. Crashing analyzes this cost trade-off.

The crashing procedure is to identify the least cost method of reducing the duration of activities on the critical path one time unit at a time. The critical path here is A–B–D. Actually, in this problem, there is only one activity that can be accomplished faster than the original schedule— activity B. The next least cost method is a fast boat, which costs $300, versus the slow boat cost of $100, for a marginal added cost of $200. This would reduce the duration of activity B to 6, resulting in the following critical path schedule (Table 3.3).

Table 3.3 Revised schedule

Activity	Duration (days)	Pred	Early start	Early finish	Late start	Late finish	Slack
A Get import license	5	None	0	5	0	5	0
B Ship	6	A	5	11	5	11	0
C Train Users	11	None	0	11	0	11	0
D Train on System	2	B,C	11	13	11	13	0

The schedule for this revision is shown in Figure 3.3.

		D	A	Y	S									
Activity	Duration	1	2	3	4	5	6	7	8	9	10	11	12	13
A license	5 d													
B **slow boat**	6 d													
C train users	11 d													
D train on system	2 d													
	Scheduled													
	Slack	s												
	Critical													

Figure 3.3 Revised schedule

This new schedule saves $500 in penalties, at an added cost of $200, for a net savings of $300. This is clearly superior to the original schedule. The difference between this schedule and the original schedule is that activity B has been crashed one day. Another result is that now all four activities are critical (all have zero slack). Looking at the network, we can see that there are now two critical paths: A–B–D and C–D. This means that if we want to reduce the project completion time, we will have to shorten both critical paths in parallel. While it is possible to reduce the original critical path A–B–D by adopting the bush airplane option, this will do nothing to reduce the new critical path, C–D. Therefore, there are no savings in penalties, whereas there is an added cost of $100 by moving from the fast boat to the bush plane. Thus, we would not be interested in further crashing the project, but would adopt the fast boat shipping option.

Crashing can also be applied to identify a cost–time trade-off. The following example (Table 3.4) demonstrates this concept.

Table 3.4 Second crashing project

Activity	Duration (days)	Pred	Early start	Early finish	Late start	Late finish	Slack	Crash
A Develop layout	19	none	0	19	0	19	0	
B Obtain permits	5	A	19	24	19	24	0	10,000/day 1 max
C Facility work	30	B	24	54	24	54	0	3,000/day 2 max
D Inspect cabling	2	C	54	56	54	56	0	
E Install remote line	53	None	0	53	0	54	0	5,000/day 12 max
F Test lines	2	E	53	55	54	56	0	
G Test system	2	D, F	56	58	56	58	0	

The network for this project is shown in Figure 3.4.

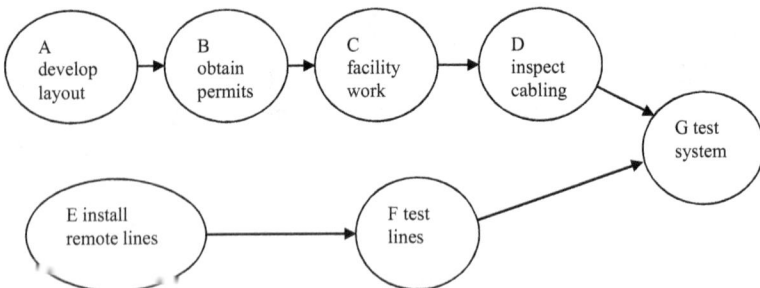

Figure 3.4 Network for line project

The schedule is shown in Figure 3.5.

Activity	Duration	D	A	Y	S	..	10	..	19	20	..	24	25	..	53	54	55	56	57	58
		1	2	3	4															
A	19 d																			
B	5 d																			
C	30 d																			
D	2 d																			
E	53 d															s				
F	2 d																	s		
G	2 d																			
	Scheduled																			
	Slack	S																		
	Critical																			

Figure 3.5 *Schedule for second crashing example*

The original critical path model requires 58 days to complete. This is with no extra costs for crashing.

The next step is to identify critical activities that can be crashed. If more than one critical path exists, all critical paths must be reduced by the same amount. In our case, there is one critical path: A–B–C–D–G. Of these critical activities, B and C can be crashed. The least expensive would be selected. In this case, that is C (at $3,000/day as opposed to $10,000/day for B).

By crashing C one day at a cost of $3,000, we can complete the project in 57 days (see Table 3.5).

Table 3.5 *Second crashing project after crashing C*

Activity	Duration (days)	Pred	Early start	Early finish	Late start	Late finish	Slack	Crash
A Develop layout	19	none	0	19	0	19	0	
B Obtain permits	5	A	19	24	19	24	0	10,000/day 1 max
C Facility work	29	B	24	53	24	53	0	3,000/day 1 max
D Inspect cabling	2	C	53	55	53	55	0	
E Install remote lines	53	None	0	53	0	53	0	5,000/day 12 max
F Test lines	2	E	53	55	53	55	0	
G Test system	2	D, F	55	57	55	57	0	

The schedule after crashing activity C is shown in Figure 3.6.

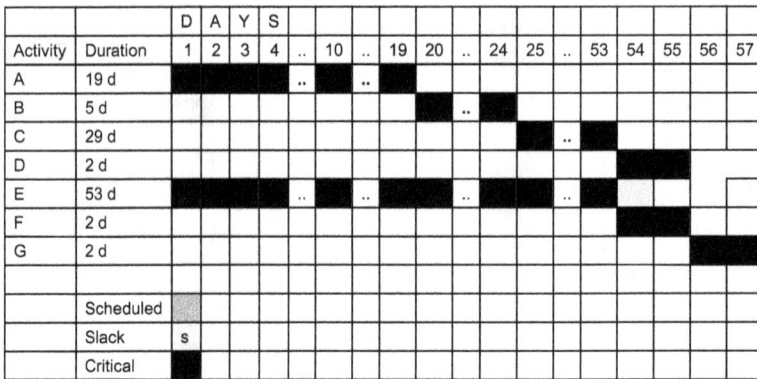

Activity	Duration	D	A	Y	S	..	10	..	19	20	..	24	25	..	53	54	55	56	57
		1	2	3	4														
A	19 d																		
B	5 d																		
C	29 d																		
D	2 d																		
E	53 d																		
F	2 d																		
G	2 d																		
	Scheduled																		
	Slack	s																	
	Critical																		

Figure 3.6 Schedule after crashing C

Now there are two critical paths: A–B–C–D–G and E–F–G. On the first path, our choices for crashing are B and C, with C still the least cost option at $3,000/day. On the second critical path, the only activity that can be crashed is E, at a cost of $5,000/day. If G had been crashable, it would have served for both critical paths, because it is an element of both. However, if G is not available (and it is not), we must crash two activities, in this case C and E, at a total cost of $8,000. This yields a solution (Table 3.6) completing the project in 56 days at an added cumulative cost of $11,000 (including the $3,000 spent to get to 57 days).

Table 3.6 Second crashing project after crashing C and E

Activity	Duration (days)	Pred	Early start	Early finish	Late start	Late finish	Slack	Crash
A Develop layout	19	none	0	19	0	19	0	
B Obtain permits	5	A	19	24	19	24	0	10,000/day 1 max
C Facility work	28	B	24	52	24	52	0	
D Inspect cabling	2	C	52	54	52	54	0	
E Install remote line	52	None	0	52	0	52	0	5,000/day 11 max
F Test lines	2	E	52	54	52	54	0	
G Test system	2	D, F	54	56	54	56	0	

We have trimmed both critical paths. All activities remain critical, and there are two critical paths: A–B–C–D–G and E–F–G. We have now exhausted the days we can crash on activity C, so our only option now is to reduce activity B to 4 days by spending another $10,000, at the same time that we reduce activity E to 51 days at an added cost of $5,000. This would reduce the project duration to 55 days (Table 3.7), at a cumulative cost of $26,000.

Table 3.7 Third crashing project after crashing B, C, and E twice

Activity	Duration (days)	Pred	Early start	Early finish	Late start	Late finish	Slack	Crash
A Develop layout	19	None	0	19	0	19	0	
B Obtain permits	4	A	19	23	19	23	0	
C Facility work	28	B	23	51	23	51	0	
D Inspect cabling	2	C	51	53	51	53	0	
E Install remote line	51	None	0	51	0	51	0	5,000/day 10 max
F Test lines	2	E	51	53	51	53	0	
G Test system	2	D, F	53	55	53	55	0	

At this stage, we can no longer reduce the duration of the critical path chain A–B–C–D–G, and so we must stop. The table of trade-offs resulting from our analysis is given in Table 3.8:

Table 3.8 Crashing options

Original schedule	58 days	No extra expenditure ($)
Crash C 1 day	57 days	3,000 extra cost
Crash C 2 days, E 1 day	56 days	11,000 extra cost
Crash B 1 day, C 2 days, E 2 days	55 days	26,000 extra cost

In this case, we do not have a benefit given for saving a day of project time. This is often the case. Managers are provided with the expected cost for a given project duration. Managers seeking the lowest expected cost would risk the 58-day plan. More cautious managers may want to spend the extra money to save time or to increase the cushion for project completion.

Summary

Often projects encounter optional means to accomplish activities. Each probably has a different cost, so project planning involves identification of a plan to accomplish the project at maximum revenue (or for government projects, minimum cost). Crashing is identifying how the project can be accomplished faster at a cost. If a project falls behind, crashing can be applied to evaluate alternatives available. Usually, there is a cost–time trade-off involved. Activities might be sped up through overtime, subcontracting, or hiring more personnel. Brooks' Law, of course, pointed out that hiring more in information systems contexts may actually slow the project, making that approach suspect in that environment. On the other hand, in construction, more shovels can usually dig more ditches faster.

PMBOK Items Relating to Chapter 3

11.5 Plan Risk Responses—Develop alternative actions to respond to eventuation of project risk elements.

Thought questions

1. Why is it necessary to iterate time period by time period when crashing a critical path?
2. How does the concept of optimality enter into crashing as presented? Are there risks in this approach?

CHAPTER 4

Probabilistic Scheduling Models

Key points:

- Activity durations usually involve high levels of uncertainty.
- Program Evaluation and Review Technique (PERT) assumes a particular form of duration distribution.
- Monte Carlo simulation is a much better approach, allowing any duration distribution.

In the last chapter, critical path models were discussed. The critical path method has been useful in project management planning and control. But it is widely recognized that the assumed durations of activities very often turn out to be different from those assumed in the planning stage. In this chapter, we will look at two types of project scheduling models that consider some of the uncertainty involved in project management. The Program Evaluation and Review Technique (PERT) assumes a beta distribution for project durations, which in itself is not necessarily realistic. PERT can easily be implemented on a spreadsheet. Simulation can be used to model projects with uncertain durations on a spreadsheet. Any realistic distribution can be modeled using simulation. While more flexible than PERT, simulation analysis of projects involves more complications than PERT.

PERT

The PERT method is a modification of the critical path method, where uncertainty in activity durations can be considered. Three estimates of activity durations are required: minimum, most likely, and maximum. The most likely estimate is relatively easy. The minimum duration of an activity also might be fairly easy to identify—the length of time the activity would take if everything went right. The third estimate, the maximum duration, is often difficult for estimators. The longest any activity can take is infinity, never finishing. However, the method won't work with that. What is meant by "maximum" is the activity duration if everything went wrong but the activity was completed regardless. When PERT is used, clear definitions of what is meant by minimum and maximum duration need to be specified. Many different variants are used.

Consider a problem of installing a new software for an element of an institution. The activities and expected times are as shown in Table 4.1:

Table 4.1 Demonstration project input

Activity	Duration (months)	Predecessors
A Requirements analysis	3	none
B Programming	7	A
C Hardware acquisition	3	A
D User training	12	A
E Implementation	5	B,C
F Testing	1	E

Figure 4.1 gives the network for this project.

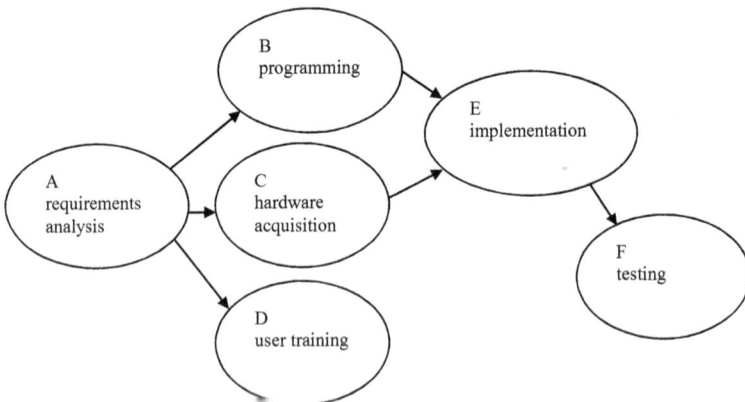

Figure 4.1 Network for demonstration project

The critical path schedule would be as shown in Table 4.2 (asterisks are given for zero slacks, indicating critical activities):

Table 4.2 Critical path schedule for demonstration project

Activity	Early start	Early finish	Late finish	Late start	Slack
A	0	3	3	0	0*
B	3	10	10	3	0*
C	3	6	10	7	4
D	3	15	16	4	1
E	10	15	15	10	0*
F	15	16	16	15	0*

The critical path in this case is the chain of activities A–B–E–F, a unique path, with an expected duration of 16 months. The PERT model is the same (Table 4.3), except that three duration estimates are used instead of one. Given these three estimates, the expected duration is given by the formula:

$$\text{expected duration} = \frac{a + 4m + b}{6}$$

Where a is the minimum estimated duration, m is the most likely duration, and b is the maximum estimated duration. The variance of the duration of any activity is also a function of these estimates (calculations in Table 4.3):

$$\text{variance} = \left(\frac{b - a}{6}\right)^2$$

Table 4.3 Calculation of activity durations and variances

Activity	Min	Likely	Max	Expected duration	Activity variance
A Requirements analysis	2	3	4	3	4/36
B Programming	6	7	9	7.17	9/36
C Hardware acquisition	3	3	3	3	0
D Train users	12	12	12	12	0
E Implementation	3	5	7	5	16/36
F Testing	1	1	2	1.17	1/36

The variance of an activity with no uncertainty, such as for activity C, is 0. The expected duration is used as the duration in a critical path analysis (Table 4.4):

Table 4.4 PERT schedule for demonstration project

Activity	Expected Duration	Predecessors	Early Start	Early Finish	Late Start	Late Finish	Slack
A	3	none	0	3	0	3	0*
B	7.17	A	3	10.17	3	10.17	0*
C	3	A	3	6	7.17	10.17	4.17
D	12	A	3	15	4.33	16.33	1.33
E	5	B,C	10.17	15.17	10.17	15.17	0*
F	1.17	E	15.17	16.33	15.17	16.33	0*

The variance of the project can be calculated as the sum of the variances of the chain of critical activities (Table 4.5):

Table 4.5 Calculation of project variance

Activity	Maximum	Minimum	Variance
A	4	2	0.111
B	9	6	0.25
E	7	3	0.444
F	2	1	0.028
Project variance			0.833

This yields a project standard deviation (square root of the variance) of 0.913. Since the durations were beta distributed, the project duration is assumed to be normally distributed. The probability of completing the project on or before any particular target time can be calculated using the Z formula.

$$z = \frac{x - \mu}{s}$$

To calculate the probability of finishing in x months, $z = (x - 16.333)/0.913$. The probability can be obtained by referring to a normal distribution or by using the NORM.S.DIST(z) function in Excel. Table 4.6 displays the probabilities of completing the project on or before the given duration.

Table 4.6 Probability calculations

Duration		z	Probability
15	(15 − 16.33)/0.913 =	−1.461	0.072
16	(16 − 16.33)/0.913 =	−0.365	0.357
17	(17 − 16.33)/0.913 =	0.73	0.767
18	(18 − 16.33)/0.913 =	1.826	0.966
19	(19 − 16.33)/0.913 =	2.921	0.998
20	(20 − 16.33)/0.913 =	4.017	0.999+

In these calculations, the variances of activities C and D were disregarded, because they had slack. If activities C or D were to experience delay, while the other activities were closer to their expected durations, this could also delay the project. If activity D were to be delayed over 2 months, for instance, it would most likely delay the overall project completion. However, this possibility is disregarded with PERT. Here, activities C and D are estimated as constants, with no expected delay. They still could become critical if activities A or B were early for some reason.

Criticisms of PERT

PERT was developed in the 1950s for the U.S. Navy. It is theoretically attractive in that it addresses an obvious limitation of the critical path method. However, it is not widely used in practice, and when it is, the minimum durations are often casual estimates, such as one-half of the expected duration, and the maximum duration is stated as twice the expected duration. When this type of input is entered, there is obvious degradation of the quality of the analysis, with no thought given to specific activity variance. Microsoft Project uses the term PERT as a label for their network diagram. (Microsoft Project does provide support to apply PERT analysis, although not on its featured menu.)

PERT is biased toward giving overly optimistic schedule estimates owing to failure to consider time delays due to interaction of noncritical activities with critical activities. The beta distribution used in the PERT method is appropriate only in the symmetric case, with the most likely time the exact mean of the minimum and maximum times, when the most likely time is about 40 percent of the distance from the minimum to the maximum, and when the most likely time is about 60 percent of the distance from the minimum to the maximum. All other cases of the beta distribution lead to some error in the PERT duration calculation.

There is also a very real problem of obtaining multiple estimates of duration. Projects are one-time affairs, and there is not a lot of data on which duration estimates can be based. Estimators have a great deal of trouble developing the most likely duration estimate and quite often resort to quick-and-dirty estimates of the minimum and most likely estimates (such as the minimum = one-half of the most likely, and the maximum = twice the most likely).

The PERT method is also based on independence of activity durations. However, this is not true in projects, as if one activity is late, there is a tendency for management to rush the ensuing activities to compensate. This would result in a case of negative correlation between durations. There can also be similar underlying causes of lateness that might be positively correlated, such as skill shortages.

Simulation for Project Scheduling

Simulation is a very valuable tool for analyzing models involving elements described by probability distributions. Projects involve interrelated activities, many of which are probabilistic. This class of problems is very easily modeled on spreadsheets, such as Excel.

Excel Simulation Model

The software installation example scheduled earlier involved six activities, A through F. Assume that the durations of some of these activities, for instance A, B, E, and F, involve some uncertainty. The best way to proceed is to gather statistics on past projects (if possible) so that sound data can be used to estimate the expected durations and probability distribution for specific activities. For the purposes of demonstration, assume that the data for these four activities was found to be normally distributed (a possibility, although certainly not the only possible appropriate distribution).

The Excel CPM model is used as the basis for a simulation of this problem. We will use column A of a spreadsheet to list the six activities.

Following the critical path spreadsheet model form from Chapter 6, we use column B for start times for each activity and column E for finish times. We reserve two columns (C and D) to generate simulated durations. We use the first of these columns (C) to generate a normally distributed random number and column D to convert the random numbers in column C to the appropriate outcomes reflecting simulated durations in column D.

In column B, the early start for any activities without predecessors is assigned the value of time 0. In this model, only activity A has no predecessor. Other cells in column B give maximum finish times values (column E) for all predecessors. Uncertain events are generated using random numbers in Excel. There are a number of ways to generate random numbers in Excel. The function: =**RAND**() returns a uniform random number between zero and one, which changes every time an action is executed in Excel. This uniform random number can be transformed into other distributions, but this operation requires more advanced study (see Evans and Olson, 1998). A second way to generate random numbers within Excel is through the **Data Analysis Toolpak** on the **Tools** menu of the Excel command ribbon. From the Data Analysis Toolpak menu, select **Random Number Generator**. The window given in Figure 4.2 is obtained.

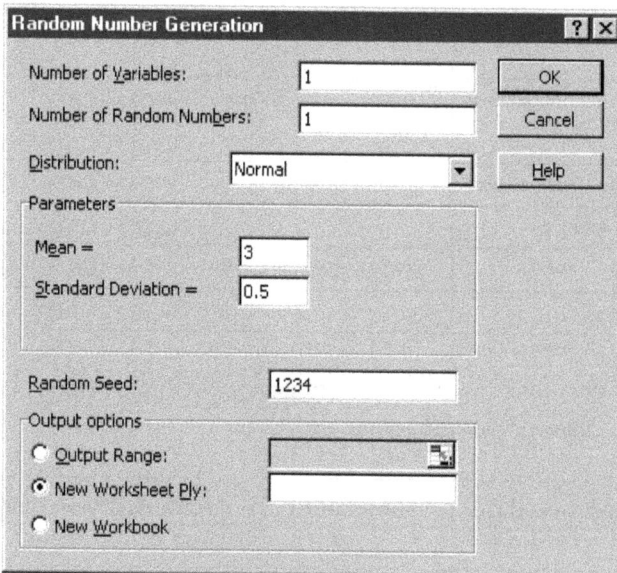

Figure 4.2 Excel random number generation window

In the following example, data was normally distributed in the four random durations modeled in cells **C2**, **C3**, **C6**, and **C7**. The Random Number Generator procedure in Excel requires the following information (Figure 4.3):

Number of Variables	the number of columns of random numbers requested
Number of Random Numbers	the number of rows of random numbers requested
Distribution	from the menu, select **Normal**
Mean	enter the random variable mean
Standard Deviation	enter the standard deviation of the random variable
Seed?	You can set a seed that will return the same sequence of random numbers

Figure 4.3 Excel random number generator information

In this example, random numbers were generated one by one. For each random number, the **Number of** Variables was set to 1, and the **Number of Random Numbers** was set to 1. A seed was not used in the example below, but seeds can be very useful in controlling experiments, making it possible to replicate the sequence of random numbers to make comparison simulation experiments easier to analyze. Specifying seeds is shown in Figure 4.2. Results are shown in Table 4.7:

Table 4.7 Excel spreadsheet of simulation model

	A	B	C	D	E
1		Start	Random	Duration	Finish
2	Requirements analysis	0	Toolpak	=IF(C2>0,C2,1)	=B2+D2
3	Programming	=E2	Toolpak	=IF(C3>0,C3,1)	=B3+D3
4	Hardware acquisition	=E2	3	=IF(C4>0,C4,1)	=B4+D4
5	User training	=E2	12	=IF(C5>0,C5,1)	=B5+D5
6	Implementation	=MAX(E3,E4)	Toolpak	=IF(C6>0,C6,1)	=B6+D6
7	Testing	=E6	Toolpak	=IF(C7>0,C7,1)	=B7+D7

The durations in column C are generated from Analysis Toolpak, using the following distributions.

Duration	cell C2	=normal(3,0.5)	from Analysis Toolpak
	cell C3	=normal(7,1)	from Analysis Toolpak
	cell C6	=normal(5,1)	from Analysis Toolpak
	cell C7	=normal(1,0.5)	from Analysis Toolpak

Column D is used to ensure that durations less than one time period are not included. Any minimum could be used for any activity. The formulation above yields the numbers in Table 4.8:

Table 4.8 Excel simulation output

	A	B	C	D	E
1		Start	Random	Duration	Finish
2	Requirements analysis	0	3.47987	3.47987	3.47987
3	Programming	3.47987	6.9808	6.9808	10.46067
4	Hardware acquisition	3.47987	3	3	6.47987
5	User training	3.47987	12	12	15.47987
6	Implementation	10.46067	5.06744	5.06744	15.52811
7	Testing	15.52811	1.36085	1.36085	16.88896

Column D could also be used to convert durations to integer values if that would be more appropriate. Cell D2, for instance, could be:

$$=INT(IF(C2>1,C2,1)+0.5)$$

The 0.5 is added to round the value generated by Excel. This yields Table 4.9:

Table 4.9 Rounding Excel output

	A	B	C	D	E
1		Start	Random	Duration	Finish
2	Requirements analysis	0	3.47987	3	3
3	Programming	3	6.9808	7	10
4	Hardware acquisition	3	3	3	6
5	User training	3	12	12	15
6	Implementation	10	5.06744	5	15
7	Testing	15	1.36085	1	16

This provides more realistic scheduling simulations if complete time units are more appropriate.

Generating Multiple Simulation Runs

The benefit of simulation is that the experiment can be repeated many times so that patterns can be identified from the set of possible outcomes generated by the simulation. Multiple simulation runs can be obtained in a number of ways, four of which are discussed here. The hard way (1) is to generate results one by one. The easy way (2) is to use simulation add-ins, such as @RISK or CRYSTAL BALL. Within Excel, multiple simulations, each with different results, can be obtained using random numbers generated by the Data Analysis Toolpak (3), but this requires the use of VISUAL BASIC. A fourth procedure (4) works using the RAND() function, although random numbers cannot be controlled with this method. Methods (3) and (4) are demonstrated in the Appendix to Chapter 7.

In the short example last demonstrated, based on 100 runs, the mean project completion time was 16.85 months, with a minimum of 10.15 months and a maximum of 29.86 months. The distributions used in this case were all normal. The sum of critical variances is 3.0, so there was more dispersion than there was in the PERT model. There may be even more variance (depending on the probability distributions used), as occasionally noncritical activities will become critical in the simulation. The standard deviation of the simulated project completion time was 4.04 months. Activity D, which had slack in CPM and PERT models, was critical over 25 percent of the time in the simulated runs and thus delayed project completion time in those cases.

The percentile values for expected project completion time appeared to be symmetric, so we can apply the normal distribution, obtaining the following probabilities of project completion by the following times. The corresponding PERT probabilities are given for comparison in Table 4.10. The simulation has much more dispersion, owing to the higher variances of inputs used.

Table 4.10 PERT comparisons

Months	Z	Cumulative probability	PERT probability
16	$(16 - 16.853)/4.045 = 0.416$	0.416	0.359
15	$(15 - 16.853)/4.045 = 0.458$	0.324	0.073
17	$(17 - 16.853)/4.045 = 0.514$	0.514	0.768
18	$(18 - 16.853)/4.045 = 0.613$	0.613	0.966
19	$(19 - 16.853)/4.045 = 0.702$	0.702	0.998
20	$(20 - 16.853)/4.045 = 0.778$	0.782	0.0001

The simulation output implies a much more distinct possibility that the project could take longer than does the PERT output. We can see that there is a.416 probability of completing the project within 16 months, but the 95th percentile was just over 24 months (obtained by identifying the 95th longest simulated time). With PERT's assumptions, the 95th percentile was below 18 months.

PERT addresses the widely recognized uncertainty involved in project management activities but makes a rigid assumption about the distribution of durations, and the calculation of probability of completion by a specified time disregards noncritical activities. Simulation provides a flexible means to evaluate the probability of projects being completed by specific times. Any distribution of duration can be assumed. The distribution used should be based on empirical data if possible. All activity paths are considered in the simple spreadsheet network. For instance, observed data may not be symmetric. The triangular distribution might provide a better fit to such data than does the normal distribution.

Scheduling Example

A firm is implementing a new information technology project to support production operations. This project requires coordination of delivery of materials and equipment, as well as development of a new personnel team. A simple critical path model of the operation consists of the following activities, predecessor relationships, and durations (Table 4.11).

Table 4.11 **CPM model**

Label	Activity	Predecessors	Durations (min, mode, max)
A	Select raw materials (by bid)	None	(3,3,5)
B	Select and receive equipment	None	(4,5,8)
C	Computer system design	None	(5,7,10)
D	Select shipping for raw materials	A	1
E	Hire and train personnel	B	2
F	Computer training program	C,E	(3,3,4)
G	Test run	D,F	1

Some of these activity durations involve uncertainty. The best guess of management (based on experience and judgment) includes triangularly distributed data for these uncertain events, measured in weeks. The network for this model is given in Figure 4.4:

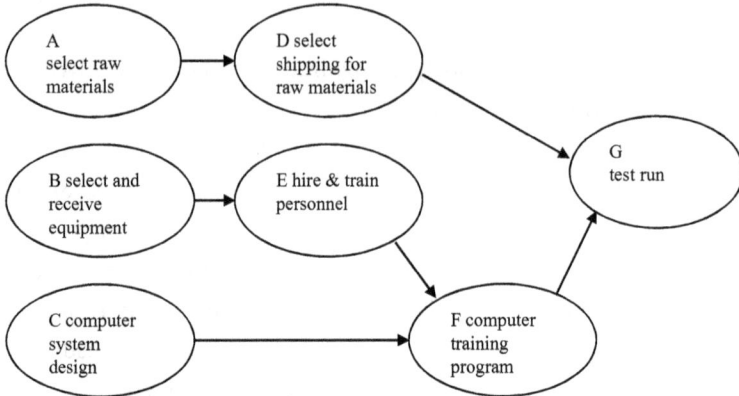

Figure 4.4 Network for scheduling example

An Excel model is given in the following table. Those durations that are not constant are drawn from the triangular distribution. The full formula is given in cell **F2**. The formula looks imposing but is simply a contingent formula based on two abutting triangles. This same formula is needed in cells **F3**, **F4**, and **F7**, differing only in that the row reference changes (in our table, the full formulation for these cells is not included). The final duration of the project appears in cell **H8**, which is the concluding activity of the project. Columns **G** and **H** implement the network model. Column **G** assigns the start times, equal to the maximum finish time of all predecessor activities. Column **H** calculates activity finish time by adding the duration to the start time. Since the particular observation for each simulation run is determined by the random numbers drawn in column **E**, each simulation run is liable to have a different critical path (see Table 4.12):

This model can be used to estimate the probability of project completion by any given time, and the distribution of project completion times can be estimated as well. Below is a run of the model (Table 4.13). The duration in this particular simulation run was 11.961, or almost 12 weeks.

Table 4.12 *Excel model formulas*

	A	B	C	D	E	F	G	H
1	Activity	Min	Mode	Max	Random	Duration	Start	Finish
2	A select raw materials	3	3	5	=RAND()	=IF(E2<=(C2-B2)/(D2-B2),B2+SQRT((C2-B2)*(D2-B2)*E2),D2-SQRT((D2-C2)*(D2-B2)*(1-E2)))	0	=G2+F2
3	B select and receive equipment	4	5	8	=RAND()	Triangular function (3)	0	=G3+F3
4	C computer system design	5	7	10	=RAND()	Triangular function (4)	0	=G4+F4
5	D select shipping for raw materials		1			=D6	=H2	=G5+F5
6	E hire and train personnel		2			=D7	=H3	=G6+F6
7	F computer training program	3	3	4	=RAND()	Triangular function (7)	=MAX(H4,H6)	=G7+F7
8	G test run		1			=D9	=MAX(H5,H7)	=G8+F8

Table 4.13 Excel numbers

	A	B	C	D	E	F	G	H
1	Activity	Min	Mode	Max	Random	Duration	Start	Finish
2	A select raw materials (by bid)	3	3	5	0.728	3.956	0	3.956
3	B select and receive equipment (fob plant)	4	5	8	0.447	5.423	0	5.423
4	C computer system design	5	7	10	0.583	7.498	0	7.498
5	D select shipping for raw materials		1			1	3.956	4.956
6	E hire and train personnel		2			2	5.423	7.423
7	F computer training program	3	3	4	0.711	3.463	7.498	10.961
8	G test run		1			1	10.961	11.961

Note that in this case fractional weeks are modeled. If desired, integer values can be obtained as demonstrated earlier. For instance, in column **F**, duration can be defined as: =INT(IF(...)+.99), which would round fractional durations up.

The results of multiple repetitions of the simulation model can be used to define a distribution of project completion times. The calculation of probability is very simple. If 100 repetitions are generated, divide the number of observed occurrences by the total number of simulation runs. The 100 results in tabular form yielded the probabilities given in Table 4.b, which are compared with the probabilities obtained from PERT for the critical path BEFG, which had a mean time of 11.5 weeks, and a standard deviation of 0.6872 weeks. In this case, specific probabilities for each range as given below are reported, as opposed to cumulative probabilities used earlier.

Table 4.14 Model results

Range	Occurrences	Probability	PERT probability
Below 10 weeks	0	0.00	0.03
Between 10 and 10.5 weeks	2	0.02	0.06
Between 10.5 and 11 weeks	2	0.02	0.14
Between 11 and 11.5 weeks	10	0.10	0.27
Between 11.5 and 12 weeks	18	0.18	0.27
Between 12 and 12.5 weeks	21	0.21	0.16
Between 12.5 and 13 weeks	17	0.17	0.06
Between 13 and 13.5 weeks	17	0.17	0.01
Between 13.5 and 14 weeks	12	0.12	0.00
Over 14 weeks (<14.5)	1	0.01	0.00

We can see that the expected project duration is almost certain to exceed 10 weeks (with a 0.96 probability of exceeding 11 weeks) and will very likely be completed within 14 weeks. But there is a lot of variance between these limits. There is a 0.28 probability that the project will take between 11 and 12 weeks, a 0.38 probability that it will take between 12 and 13 weeks, and a 0.30 probability that it will take over 13 weeks. These results demonstrate the theoretical bias of PERT to be below the true values. Simulation provides output that enables interpretation of probability for any particular duration or range. Relying on sampling theory, the degree of accuracy of these estimates is a matter of the number of samples (runs) taken.

Summary

Project management techniques have proven very useful in the planning and control of interrelated activities, but the durations of projects is notoriously variable. CPM and PERT are very useful in analyzing the interrelationships among activities, but CPM assumes constant durations, and while PERT allows a specific type of duration distribution, this particular distribution is not always appropriate, and PERT includes other inaccuracies.

Simulation of project management problems is much more flexible. Whatever distributions of expected times are appropriate can be entered into a simulation model. Simulation analysis is very flexible as well. Analysis in much greater detail is possible with simulation than is possible with PERT, although simulation requires more in the way of statistical analysis to interpret output. The mean values of simulation output provide the same information as CPM, and a more complete probabilistic output is obtained with simulation than is available from PERT.

PMBOK Items Relating to Chapter 4

11.1 Plan Risk Management—develop alternative plans to respond to project delays.

11.2 Identify Risks—process of determining which risks may affect the project and documenting their characteristics.

11.3 Perform Qualitative Risk Analysis—process of prioritizing risks for further analysis or action by assessing and combining their probability of occurrence and impact.

11.4 Perform Quantitative Risk Analysis—process of numerically analyzing the effect of identified risks on overall project objectives.

11.5 Plan Risk Responses—process of developing options and actions to enhance opportunities and to reduce threats to project objectives.

11.6 Implement Risk Responses—process of dealing with risk issues as they arise.

11.7 Monitor Risks—process of auditing project quality performance.

Thought questions

1. What are limitations of the PERT method?
2. How does Monte Carlo simulation overcome some PERT limitations?
3. What is a random number?
4. What kinds of software are available to support Monte Carlo simulation?

CHAPTER 5

Critical Chain Project Management

Key points:
- Buffers provide a means to apply bottleneck concepts to project management.
- The critical chain process is described.
- Various buffers are defined and demonstrated.
- Fever charts are presented for possible use in project control.

Critical chain project management (CCPM) has become a research area, applying the ideas developed by Goldratt.[1] The gist is that care should be applied to bottleneck activities (critical activities) and buffers applied to obtain assurance of completion of those critical activities on time.

Buffers

The primary means to ensure that critical activities are completed on time is to use buffers. A buffer is time that is included in the schedule to protect against unanticipated delays and to allow early starts. Buffers are different from slack. Slack is spare time. Buffers are time blocks that are not expected to be used for work time (the same as slack) but are dedicated to cover most likely contingencies and are closely watched so that if they are not needed, subsequent activities can proceed at the earliest time possible. **Project buffers** are used after the final task of a project to protect project completion time from delays. **Feeding buffers** are placed at each point where a non-critical activity is related to a critical path activity. Feeding buffers protect the critical activities from tasks that precede them and allow for early starts of critical activities. **Resource buffers** are placed before resources that are scheduled to work on critical activities to ensure that resources will be available and that their shortage will not delay critical activities. Resource buffers can be implemented by either issuing warning notices to those managing the resource ahead of the required time or scheduling a time to mobilize the resource as a predecessor to the critical activity using it. In multiple project environments, **strategic resource buffers** can be used to ensure that key resources are available for critical activities.

To demonstrate the use of buffers, consider an advertising schedule consisting of the activities given in Figure 5.1 where A (1 week) precedes B (3 weeks); B precedes C (3 weeks), D (2 weeks) and F (2 weeks); C and D precede E (1 week); and F precedes G (1 week). If the campaign had to be completed in 8 weeks, there is currently no room for a project buffer, as the chain of critical activities (activities A–B–C–E) have a planned duration of 8 weeks, equal to the available time. However, there may be ways to accomplish specific tasks at the cost of some extra effort or expenditure. For instance, it may be possible to obtain the product manager's approval in 1 week rather than the planned 3 weeks. This is an attractive activity to shorten, because it occurs early in the project, and if approval is not obtained, effort on later activities will not be wasted. The product manager may require a thorough analysis. If this thorough analysis is accomplished by working late hours during the week and working weekends, it may be possible to develop the required analysis within a week. This would allow shortening the project by 2 weeks, as the schedule in Figure 5.1 shows:

		W	E	E	K	S			
Activity	Duration	1	2	3	4	5	6	7	8
A rough design of advertising plan	1 week							b	s
B convince product manager to adopt	1 week							b	s
C develop marketing plan with staff	3 weeks							b	s
D identify media alternatives	2 weeks						s	b	s
E print materials	1 week							b	s
F brief sales force	2 weeks					s	s	b	s
G select media	1 week						s	b	s
	Scheduled								
	Slack	s							
	BUFFER	b							

Figure 5.1 Demonstration of buffer

There now are 2 weeks available to complete the project. One of these weeks can be used as a project buffer, insulating the work that needs to be done from the project deadline. (This leaves one additional week of slack for each activity, making no activities critical at this point.) Project buffer is not planned to be used, but is available should something go wrong with critical activities or with noncritical activities beyond their available slack.

Feeding buffers can be used as pseudo activities to marshal the required resources, making sure that they are available in time and that critical activities are not delayed. For instance, activity E, printing materials, is crucial. The marketing plan must be completed before printing can begin, because the marketing plan is the essence of what is to be produced. The project manager can plan on using week 6 as a buffer to ensure that all materials needed by the printer are available (Figure 5.2).

Activity	Duration	W 1	E 2	E 3	K 4	S 5	6	7	8
A rough design of advertising plan	1 week								b
B convince product manager to adopt	1 week								b
C develop marketing plan with staff	3 weeks								b
D identify media alternatives	2 weeks					s			b
E print materials	1 week						b		b
F brief sales force	2 weeks					s	s		b
G select media	1 week						s		b
	Scheduled								
	Slack	s							
	BUFFER	b							

Figure 5.2 Advertising schedule critical path

Now the critical activities reappear. Critical activities are activities without slack. All seven activities have a week of project buffer in week 8. Activity E has a week of feeding buffer in week 6, when materials are gathered to ensure that the critical printing activity will proceed as planned. There is now no slack for the chain A–B–C–E. An equivalent way to model this schedule is shown in Figure 5.3.

The critical path would now be A–B–C–CE–E. It is important that if the buffer is not needed, subsequent activities should proceed to work early. For instance, if the feeding buffer between activities C and E is not required, and all required material is ready at the beginning of week 6, printing should

		W	E	E	K	S			
Activity	Duration	1	2	3	4	5	6	7	8
A rough design of advertising plan	1 week	■							b
B convince product manager to adopt	1 week		■						b
C develop marketing plan with staff	3 weeks			■	■	■			b
D identify media alternatives	2 weeks					s			b
CE feeding buffer	1 week						b		
E print materials	1 week							■	b
F brief sales force	2 weeks					s	s		b
G select media	1 week						s		b
	Scheduled								
	Slack	s							
	Critical		b						
	BUFFER	b							

Figure 5.3 Equivalent model using feeding buffer

go ahead in week 6. If the duration of activity E is the planned 1 week, the project would then be completed by the end of week 6. If the feeding buffer CE turns out to be needed, and printing require extra time, there is project buffer available in week 8. This buffer, like all other buffers, should not be used unless necessary in light of sound management principles.

Resource buffers could be used if a key resource, such as the team that develops the advertising plan, were heavily scheduled on other activities. A resource buffer in that case would be time allocated to ensure that the key resource had time to gear up for this particular project. In construction, an obvious resource buffer could exist if there were a key piece of equipment, such as a large crane, that was very expensive and valuable for many other projects. (In this case, it would be a strategic resource buffer.) The key resource might be needed elsewhere or might be found to be across the country working on a prior project. A strategic resource buffer would then be included in the schedule to ensure that time was available to transport it, to replace it if necessary (and possible), or in case of mechanical difficulties, to repair it. The resource buffer, like all four forms of buffer, represents planning ahead for reasonable contingencies.

Critical Chain Process

We draw on Ellis[2] to describe the implementation of CCPM. The idea is to increase deficiency by minimizing multitasking and procrastination to ensure tasks are ready to start, focus on cooperative teamwork, and generate a common focus on critical tasks. The method uses what they call "aggressive duration estimates." (They assume that estimators provide conservative duration estimates, at roughly the 90th or 95th percentile of expected, which leads to waste.) The idea is that the critical chain of activities will have components that are sometimes early, sometimes late, and, rather than use the late assumption for each activity, use the most likely and add a project buffer at the end to represent project variance.

This is problematic. As someone who spent a decade estimating construction projects, and studying delays pretty thoroughly, I would dispute that you can assume this inflation on a regular basis. Duration estimates are biased, but the more experience the organization has with an activity, the less variance. That's in construction. In information systems projects, I have had a very good systems engineer tell me that when he is ever asked how long a programming activity will take, he responds, "As long as it takes to do it right." Thus the CCPM method starts with a gross assumption that makes it look like it saves a great deal of time but that I would argue leads to very dangerous scheduling. Furthermore, the assumption that there will be compensating early finishes to balance some of the late finishes is also problematic, as correlation often appears in projects.

Once a critical path network is developed, with estimated durations and resource requirements provided, the critical path is identified. Then CCPM involves the following steps:

Step 1: Remove resource constraints
All tasks using the same resource are staggered to avoid overtaxing constrained resources.

Step 2: Reduce task duration by changing certainty from 90%
 to 50%
Since the 95th percentile in a normal curve is 1.96 standard deviations from the mean, divide the original duration estimates by 2.

Step 3: Add feeder buffers
Ensure noncritical activities don't delay the critical path by adding a buffer to interfaces between them.

Step 4: User the relay-race mentality
When noncritical tasks are scheduled, delay them to start as late as possible (considering feeder buffers).

Step 5: Add a project buffer

At the end of a critical chain, add a buffer (50 percent is popular) to reflect project variance.

> If Step 5 is done, on average the CCPM duration will be about 75 percent of the traditional critical path (durations are divided by 2; then the overall critical path duration is multiplied by 1.5). This is supposed to show improved efficiency. This requires the gross assumptions discussed earlier—not all projects have the same variance. (Although CCPM proponents would rightly argue that you can adjust the project buffer accordingly, dividing the durations by two is undeniably gross). The argument is that there are behavioral biases of estimators leading to duration inflation that is counterproductive (and there is admittedly some truth to that). The student syndrome refers to a tendency among students to put off working on assignments until the last minute. Parkinson's Law is that the time taken to complete a task will tend to equal the allowed time. There is also the project feature of predecessor relationships whereby finishing early has no value (if you finish early, you just have to wait for the others).

Demonstration Model

Consider a project to install new software. Table 5.1 gives six activities with three estimates of duration in weeks and predecessor relationships (assuming a triangular distribution of durations):

The network for this model is shown in Figure 5.4:

Table 5.1 Demonstration project parameters

Code	Activity	Predecessors	Min	Mode	Max	Expected	Variance
A	Requirements analysis	None	3	4	5	4	0.1111
B	Programming	A	6	7	14	8	1.7778
C	Hardware acquisition	A	1	2	3	2	0.1111
D	Train users	A	12	12	12	12	0
E	Implementation	B,C	4	6	8	6	0.4444
F	Testing	E	1	1	7	2	1.0

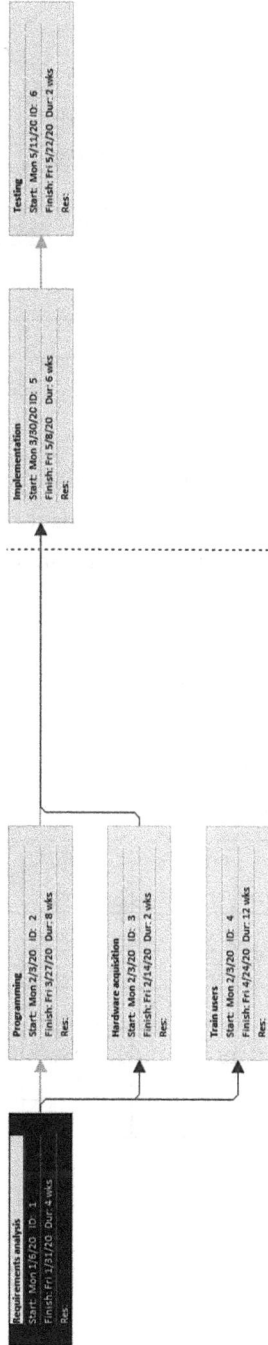

Figure 5.4 Network

Table 5.2 gives the critical path results using expected durations:

Table 5.2 Demonstration critical path schedule

Code	Expected	Predecessors	Early start	Early finish	Late start	Late finish	Slack
A	4	None	0	4	0	4	0
B	8	A	4	12	4	12	0
C	2	A	4	6	10	12	6
D	12	A	4	16	8	20	4
E	6	B,C	12	18	12	18	0
F	2	E	18	20	18	20	0

There is only one critical path. The critical path is thus A–B–E–F, with an expected completion time of 20. Variance is 0.1111 + 1.7778 + 0.4444 + 1.0 = 3.3333. This makes the standard deviation 1.8257.

There are no resources given at this stage, so the first step is not needed yet. The second step is to divide durations by 2 (Table 5.3). Note that we assume hardware acquisition duration of 2 weeks to be fixed at 2 weeks, but the other activities can be reduced:

Table 5.3 Critical path after reducing durations

Code	Expected	Predecessors	Early start	Early finish	Late start	Late finish	Slack
A	2	None	0	2	0	2	0
B	4	A	2	6	2	6	0
C	2	A	2	4	4	6	2
D	6	A	2	8	4	10	2
E	3	B,C	6	9	6	9	0
F	1	E	9	10	9	10	0

Step 3 of CCPM would be to add feeder buffers where slack activities connect with the critical path. Activity C connects with activity E. Feeder buffers, sometimes at least, are assigned as half the task's length, which for C would be 1. After this type of buffer is added, the critical path would look like Table 5.4:

Activities with feeder buffers are delayed in Step 4 to finish at their late finish. Thus, the plan now is given in Table 5.5:

Table 5.4 Critical path after feeder buffering

Code	Expected	Predecessors	Early start	Early finish	Late start	Late finish	Slack
A	2	None	0	2	0	2	0
B	4	A	2	6	2	6	0
C	2	A	2	4	3	5	1
C'	1	C	4	5	4	6	1
D	6	A	2	8	4	10	2
E	3	B,C'	6	9	6	9	0
F	1	E	9	10	9	10	0

Table 5.5 Implemented schedule

Activity	Start	Finish
A	0	2
B	2	6
C	3	5
D	2	8
E	6	9
F	9	10

Activity D could also be delayed, but that would make it critical—adding a feeder buffer would extend beyond the project. Common sense needs to be applied—it would probably be best to let D start at 2 as would conventionally be done, hoping the slack of 2 is sufficient.

Step 5 is to add a project buffer. Note that the feeder buffer timing could create a logical problem if the feeder buffer would make a slack activity extend beyond the expected project finish time of the critical chain. Step 5 is to add the project buffer, sometimes taken to be 50 percent of the project duration, which here would have been 5 weeks. This yields the CCPM schedule shown in Table 5.6:

The Program Evaluation Review Technique (PERT) schedule would have had a project duration of 20, a bit more than this schedule, which is what critical chain advocates argue you should expect—a shorter schedule with just as much if not more control. The purported value of CCPM is in project control, using fever charts to monitor progress by focusing on

Table 5.6 Critical path after project buffer

Code	Expected	Predecessors	Early start	Early finish	Late start	Late finish	Slack
A	2	None	0	2	0	2	0
B	4	A	2	6	2	6	0
C	2	A	2	4	3	5	1
C'	1	C	4	5	5	6	1
D	6	A	2	8	4	10	2
E	3	B,C'	6	9	6	9	0
F	1	E	9	10	9	10	0
ProjB	5	D,F	10	15	10	15	0

remaining project buffer. Using the PERT data, the probability of finishing in 15 weeks would be:

$z = (15 - 20)/1.8257 = -2.7387$	Probability$\{z = -2.7387\} = 0.0032$

We could also use the minimums, in line with the idea that close managerial control might speed up activities. The PERT minima yield a project completion of 14 weeks.

$z = (15 - 14)/1.8257 = 0.5477$	Probability$\{z = 0.5477\} = 0.7081$

Using the mode would yield a project completion of 18 weeks.

$z = (15 - 18)/1.8257 = -1.6432$	Probability$\{z = -1.6432\} = 0.0502$

These three calculations show how sensitive the probability is to the data. In this case, the critical chain schedule would be very ambitious. But the idea is that project management can focus on control to reduce durations. If they could effectively control the project, they would have a pretty good probability of finishing on time. If they let the project follow its course, they could be in trouble. The practicality of that idea depends a great deal on the ability to control variances. We compare that with PERT, which makes a great many assumptions of its own and in practice probably tends to inflate schedules more than needed.

Fever Charts

The key to fever charts is to compare progress against two limits. A safe region might be using less than 80 percent of buffer available compared with critical path complete. A danger region might be use of over 110 percent of available buffer compared with critical path complete. In the safe region, buffer penetration is low, and there is no perceived need to interfere with project progress. In the danger region, action is called for (motivation, crashing, or contacting project owner). In between, the project manager should consider contingent action plans if more delays are encountered.

A key calculation in a fever chart is to compare critical chain completed (equivalent to earned weeks) with time passed. The fever chart focuses on buffer penetration, which is defined as time passed minus critical chain completed. Here the critical chain is A–D–E–F. The focus is to compare buffer penetration into three areas—if buffer penetration is below an OK line, which is sometimes set at 80 percent of the critical chain path, all is well. If buffer penetration is above a Danger line, sometimes set at 110 percent of the critical chain path, drastic action is called for. Between these limits, project management is encouraged to be watchful and proactive Assume the most likely estimated durations in our example (Table 5.7) and using the critical path complete estimate of 18 weeks. The project using the modes took 18 weeks, 3 weeks over the CCPM estimate. Slack activities C and D are shown giving their proportion completed, but don't impact the fever chart. (They could disrupt project completion, however). Proportions in Table 5.7 are the proportion of the critical path earned based on CCPM estimated durations:

In Table 5.8, the mode durations from Table 5.1 are used. Here, the buffer generated by the critical chain schedule assuming sped-up durations is steadily used up, in the danger zone throughout. This is what would happen if no corrective action were taken to bring things back on schedule (through motivation or crashing or whatever means exist to speed progress in the lagging activity).

Figure 5.5 displays these results:

If, as usually occurs, things start off optimistically through analysis and programming but testing takes longer than expected, the fever chart might look quite different. A common problem is that things seem like

Table 5.7 Fever chart elements using mode

Week	A	B	C	D	E	F	OK	Danger
1	0.050	0	0	0	0	0	0.0444	0.0611
2	0.100	0	0	0	0	0	0.0889	0.1222
3	0.150	0	0	0	0	0	0.1333	0.1833
4	0.200	0	0	0	0	0	0.1778	0.2444
5		0.257	0.5	0.083	0	0	0.2222	0.3056
6		0.314	1.0	0.167	0	0	0.2667	0.3667
7		0.371		0.250	0	0	0.3111	0.4278
8		0.429		0.333	0	0	0.3556	0.4889
9		0.486		0.417	0	0	0.4000	0.5500
10		0.543		0.500	0	0	0.4444	0.6111
11		0.600		0.583	0	0	0.4889	0.6722
12				0.667	0.650	0	0.5333	0.7333
13				0.750	0.700	0	0.5778	0.7944
14				0.833	0.750	0	0.6222	0.8556
15				0.917	0.800	0	0.6667	0.9167
16				1.000	0.850	0	0.7111	0.9778
17					0.900	0	0.7556	1.0389
18						1.0	0.8000	1.1000

Table 5.8 Fever chart assuming mode performance

Week	Project	Critical path progress	Buffer used	OK	Danger
1	A	0.5	0.5	0.27	0.37
2	A	1	1	0.53	0.73
3	A	1.5	1.5	0.80	1.10
4	A	2	2	1.07	1.47
5	B	2.57	2.43	1.33	1.83
6	B	3.14	2.86	1.60	2.20
7	B	3.71	3.29	1.87	2.57
8	B	4.29	3.71	2.13	2.93
9	B	4.86	4.14	2.40	3.30
10	B	5.43	4.57	2.67	3.67
11	B	6	5	2.93	4.03
12	E	6.5	5	3.20	4.40
13	E	7	5	3.47	4.77
14	E	7.5	5	3.73	5.13
15	E	8	5	4.00	5.50
16	E	8.5	5	4.27	5.87
17	E	9	5	4.53	6.23
18	F	10	5	4.80	6.60

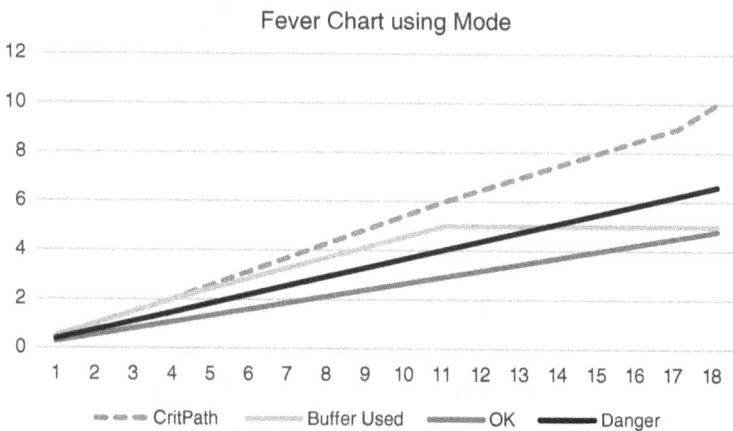

Fever Chart using Mode

Figure 5.5 Fever chart using mode durations

they are going on schedule until near the end of the activity. Let us assume that after week 5 it becomes apparent that programming will take 8 weeks rather than 4. Then assume testing takes 5 weeks rather than 1. Table 5.9 and Figure 5.6 display a line graph of the project critical chain project progress (CCC—critical path complete) through the planned 9 weeks:

Table 5.9 CCPM with late problems

Week	Project	Critical path progress	Buffer used	OK	Danger
1	A	1	0	0.27	0.37
2	A	2	0	0.53	0.73
3	B	3	0	0.80	1.10
4	B	4	0	1.07	1.47
5	B	4.5	0.5	1.33	1.83
6	B	5	1	1.60	2.20
7	B	5.3	1.7	1.87	2.57
8	B	5.6	2.4	2.13	2.93
9	B	5.8	3.2	2.40	3.30
10	B	6	4	2.67	3.67
11	E	7	4	2.93	4.03
12	E	8	4	3.20	4.40
13	E	9	4	3.47	4.77
14	F	9.2	4.8	3.73	5.13
15	F	9.5	5.5	4.00	5.50
16	F	9.7	6.3	4.27	5.87
17	F	9.9	7.1	4.53	6.23
18	F	10	8	4.80	6.60

There was no buffer penetration through 4 weeks. Then buffer is used up during programming delays through week 10, plotting in the intermediate zone in week 8 and beyond the danger zone in week 10, recovering a bit during installation. During testing, progress fell behind to cross the danger line again. By week 15 there is no way to recover as the 5-week buffer is used up. Unfortunately, the nature of software development projects is often like this programmers tend to think everything is OK

CCPM with Late Problems

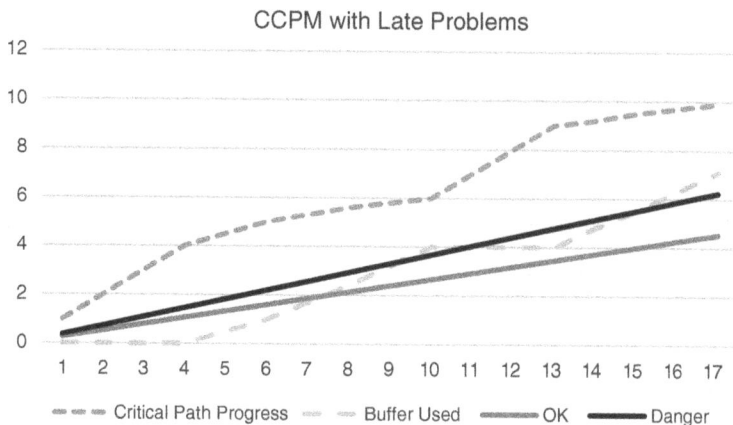

Figure 5.6 Fever chart with late delay

until late in the project. Testing is another critical area where problems are often identified.

Multiple Projects

The CCPM approach also addresses multiple projects sharing critical (bottleneck) resources. This is addressed in Step 1, but we skipped coverage until we had demonstrated the basic process of adding buffers.

Step 1 requires consideration of constrained resources. Let us presume a simple type of project with three sequential activities: Preparation–Build–Finish. Let us also assume that we have three such projects. Table 5.10 gives data, including due dates, which can be a common basis for prioritizing to stagger projects around the constrained resource. We will consider one critical resource, assuming that you can get plenty of sources to do Preparation and Building, but the Finish activities have to be done by a key professional. Note that many times you might have multiple critical resources, making the exercise even more interesting.

Table 5.10 Multiple project data

Project	Preparation	Build	Finish	Due date
P1	2 weeks	6 weeks	4 weeks	12 weeks
P2	2 weeks	2 weeks	4 weeks	14 weeks
P3	2 weeks	2 weeks	4 weeks	16 weeks

The process for multiple projects would be:

1. Stagger the projects around the critical bottleneck resource.
2. Add a capacity buffer for bottleneck resources. It is suggested that this buffer be 50 percent of the critical task in the preceding project.
3. Add a drum buffer to ensure noncritical tasks will be ready. It is suggested that this drum buffer be 50 percent of the preceding noncritical task in the prior project, added to the end of the noncritical task.

For the data in Table 5.10, the critical path model would be as shown in Table 5.11, reducing task durations by dividing by 2:

Table 5.11 Multiple project critical path

Activity	Duration	Predecessors	Early start	Early finish	Late start	Late Finish	Slack
P1 Prep	1	None	0	1	0	1	0
P1 Build	3	P1 Prep	1	4	1	4	0
P1 Finish	2	P1 Build	4	6	4	6	0
P2 Prep	1	None	0	1	4	5	4
P2 Build	1	P2 Prep	1	2	5	6	4
P2 Finish	2	P2 Build, P1 Finish	6	8	6	8	0
P3 Prep	1	None	0	1	6	7	6
P3 Build	1	P3 Prep	1	2	7	8	6
P3 Finish	2	P3 Build, P2 Finish	8	10	8	10	0

Thus to review the process:

Step 1: Remove the resource constraint by staggering project Finish schedules around the critical resource of the Finisher (Table 5.12):

Step 2: Divide durations by 2 (Table 5.13). Note that you can apply judgment as to how much to change durations rather than literally dividing each estimated duration by 2.

Here, the critical path is Project 1 Prep, Project 1 Build, Project 1 Finish, Project 2 Finish, and Project 3 Finish, shown in bold.

Table 5.12 Remove resource constraint

Week	1	2	3	4	5	6	7	8	9	10	11	12	13	14	15	16	17	18	19	20
Project 1	Pr	Pr	Bd	Bd	Bd	Bd	Bd	Bd	Fin	Fin	Fin	Fin								
Project 2			Pr	Pr	Bd	Bd							Fin	Fin	Fin	Fin				
Project 3					Pr	Pr	Bd	Bd									Fin	Fin	Fin	Fin

Table 5.13 Adjust durations

Week	1	2	3	4	5	6	7	8	9	10
Project 1	Pr	Bd	Bd	Bd	Fin	Fin				
Project 2		Pr			Bd		Fin	Fin		
Project 3			Pr			Bd			Fin	Fin

Step 3: Add capacity buffer for the critical resource. This would involve two following Finish activities. Capacity buffer (CB) duration of 50 percent would amount to one week each (Table 5.14):

Table 5.14 Addition of capacity buffer

Week	1	2	3	4	5	6	7	8	9	10	11	12
Project 1	Pr	Bd	Bd	Bd	Fin	Fin						
Project 2		Pr			Bd			CB	Fin	Fin		
Project 3			Pr			Bd				CB	Fin	Fin

This would extend the project from 10 weeks (which was very optimistic) to 12 weeks.

Step 4: Use the relay-race approach, to end noncritical activities as late as possible, but adding drum buffers (DB) before the intersection of the bottleneck resource to ensure that they will be ready (Table 5.15):

Table 5.15 Application of relay-race mentality

Week	1	2	3	4	5	6	7	8	9	10	11	12
Project 1	Pr	Bd	Bd	Bd	Fin	Fin						
Project 2				Pr	Bd	DB	CB	Fin	Fin			
Project 3							Pr	Bd	DB	CB	Fin	Fin

Step 5: Add project buffer:

The project buffer is suggested to be 50 percent of the expected duration. Here, that would come out to be 6 weeks (Table 5.16):

Now the project extends to 18 weeks.

Table 5.16 *Addition of project buffer*

Week	1	2	3	4	5	6	7	8	9	10	11	12	13	14	15	16	17	18
Project 1	Pr	Bd	Bd	Bd	Fin	Fin												
Project 2				Pr	Bd	DB	CB	Fin	Fin									
Project 3							Pr	Bd	DB	CB	Fin	Fin						
Proj Buffer													PB	PB	PB	PB	PB	PB

Summary

The critical chain idea is good enough in that there is a bias toward inflation of duration estimates. However, the solution the CCPM comes up with often ends up putting the padding back. And it is a gross assumption that project estimates are double the expected. The more experience and the less risk, the lower this biased duration inflation would be. Dividing durations by two in that case would be very dangerous.

The idea of the fever chart could be a useful means of monitoring project progress. However, there is a well-known tendency for projects to appear to be fine until the bitter end, when unexpected delays are encountered. In that case, the fever chart would appear to be unable to identify trouble until too late.

PMBOK Items Relating to Chapter 5

11.1 Plan Risk Management—develop alternative plans to respond to project delays.

11.2 Identify Risks—process of determining which risks may affect the project and documenting their characteristics.

11.3 Perform Qualitative Risk Analysis—process of prioritizing risks for further analysis or action by assessing and combining their probability of occurrence and impact.

11.4 Perform Quantitative Risk Analysis—process of numerically analyzing the effect of identified risks on overall project objectives.

11.5 Plan Risk Responses—process of developing options and actions to enhance opportunities and to reduce threats to project objectives.

11.6 Implement Risk Responses—process of dealing with risk issues as they arise.

11.7 Monitor Risks—process of auditing project quality performance.

Thought questions

1. If you literally apply the critical chain process and divide durations by two, this can lead to inconsistencies. How might common sense be applied to modify this concept seeking to overcome padding on the part of estimators?

2. How can fever charts aid in control of projects? Is that similar to the concept of focusing on critical activities with related dangers?

3. What is the logic behind the relay-race mentality?

Notes

1. E.M. Goldratt. 1997. *Critical Chain*. Great Barrington, MA: North River Press.

2. G. Ellis. 2016. "Critical Chain Project Management (CCPM)" In *Project Management in Product Development: Leadership Skills and Management Techniques to Develop Great Projects* (Oxford, England: Butterworth-Heinemann).

CHAPTER 6

Project Control and Assessment

Key points:
- Projects involve many risks.
- Project control is a process of identifying problems and applying solutions.
- RACI (Responsible, Accountable, Consulted, Informed), budget, and earned value are tools to aid in project control.

Project control, like risk analysis and estimation, needs to be applied from the beginning of the project to the project's end. **Control** is concerned with keeping the project on target with respect to its objectives. Assessment is the means of monitoring project progress to identify problems requiring control action. The project, to be a success, should conform to the project plan as much as possible. Project management must adapt to new circumstances while simultaneously seeking to meet cost, time, and quality targets. This requires close coordination between the project manager and his or her superiors, whether they are part of the same organization or not.

Risk Management

We have seen that there are many potential problems that need to be anticipated in project management. There are many risks in software development projects. The actions to alleviate these risks are means of control. Actions need to be taken throughout the project, and include continual monitoring to ensure that problems do not get out of control.

Personnel Shortfalls

In the area of personnel management, one obvious approach is to obtain quality people. When operating in a matrix organization, people are obtained from the functional areas of the organization. Boehm recommended meeting with these functional managers to preschedule good people by name and documenting these agreements. If people are obtained either from a matrix organization or from outside the organization, references should be checked to improve the probability that they will fit their planned roles.

The second personnel technique is team building. Proactive efforts should be taken to see that project management and team members share objectives. Participative planning and objective setting activities are useful to attain this aim, as well as group consensus techniques. Brainstorming, the Nominal Group Technique, and Delphi methods are tools that can lead to group consensus by sharing ideas on the issue under consideration.

Controlling Dynamic Requirements

Project requirements are sometimes changed extensively. Some change needs to be accommodated, as there are inevitable environmental changes that must be adjusted for. We have stressed user involvement, but once the scope of the project has been set, additional change (what systems people call scope creep) can be very detrimental to productivity. Some projects get out of control in the sense that requirements are constantly adjusted. One response to gain control over such a situation is to have a **high change threshold**, that is, not changing plans until it is absolutely clear that this is necessary. Risks are also reduced by deferring the development of those project components that involve high probabilities of change. Another means of dealing with inevitable changes consists of determining major directions of anticipated changes in requirements and developing the system, so that only minor revisions to the system are required (only one module would need to be replaced rather than revising the entire system).

Controlling Externally Provided Project Components

Combining system components obtained from multiple sources always creates risks of compatibility. These risks can be reduced by the activities of coordination and inspection. **Reference checking** involves contacting existing users of the component in question to verify features such as ease of use, ease of change, and other critical risk factors. **Preaward audits** in the form of checklists and other techniques can be used to reduce the risk that outside vendors are incapable of delivering the component they are to provide. Other means of reducing the risk of failure in externally furnished components include use of award-fee contracts, soliciting competitive designs and prototypes, and involving outside providers in the project team.

Real-Time Performance Risk

The ability of the developed system to perform under actual working conditions is always uncertain until the system is implemented. There are a number of techniques available to reduce the risk of inadequate performance. In the context of project management, **benchmarking** involves placing the system under a representative workload and analyzing the system's ability to cope with this level of activity. Prototyping is another means of testing the critical performance features of a system. Instrumentation and tuning measure system performance in terms of bottlenecks. When bottlenecks are encountered, workload can be adjusted by changing task sequence, priorities, data distribution, and other workload characteristics to improve system performance. **Technical analysis** examines the ability of the system to function in environments such as distributed processing. The system's fault tolerance, security, and accuracy are also tested. Techniques supporting technical analysis include fault-tree analysis, and failure modes and effects analysis.

Contingent Development Methods

Software systems should deliver functions needed by users. **Incremental development** allows organizations to test the functionality of system parts without wasting money on the entire project should it prove inadequate. **Prototyping** is a useful means of verifying the functionality of systems to users. Prototyping is also good for assessing the fault tolerance of systems. As the functionality of systems components is evaluated, those that are found lacking can be eliminated by **requirements scrubbing**. Cost-benefit methods provide one basis for deciding whether to keep a system feature or not.

Mission analysis is the process of evaluating the contribution of a system component to accomplish an organizational objective. Mission analysis requires examination of the user's mission and the role of information system support in leading to successful accomplishment of those missions. One of the key factors in information system project success has been identified as a clear statement of project objectives. Mission analysis would be a way of implementing this key factor. Tools to study the user's mission include identification of user tasks, data flows, and control procedures, as well as cost-benefit analysis.

Unrealistic Estimates

Many projects suffer from difficulties in obtaining accurate estimates of cost and time in information systems projects. One approach is to design projects to the available budget. The level of delivered functionality would be a variable. Software system components could be prioritized into mandatory, desired, and optional groups. The final design would have to include mandatory items, should include desired items, and would include optional items only if adequate time and budget were available.

The Control Process

There are some fundamental differences between planning and control. Planning focuses on setting goals and directions. Control is concerned with guiding project effort toward attainment of these goals. Planning involves allocating resources to elements of the project hierarchy. Control seeks to ensure effective use of these resources. Planning requires anticipation of problems. Control requires correction of problems. Planning is a motivational effort, while control is more a matter of rewarding achievement.

Control requires understanding what is going on with a project. Project managers need to visit operations, and see for themselves what is going on. Many actual problems do not show up in reports until it is too late for effective corrective action to be taken. Furthermore, a sense of the morale of members of the project team is better gained by actual visits.

Visits, in turn, do not reveal details about performance that reports can. Reports of project progress should be as accurate as possible. Reports are used in a control sense by providing concrete measures of actual versus planned accomplishments of technical activities. Both time and cost reports are crucial to give the project manager a clear picture of project performance. Major variances need to be understood by the project manager. There could be reasons beyond the control of anyone connected with the project. On the other hand, they could be the result of things that the project management team could correct. These variances also trigger a need for overall management to decide whether the project should be continued or dropped.

There are three general phases of the control process. **Performance standards** are set at the beginning of the project. These provide technical specifications, budgeted costs, schedules, and resource requirements. Source documents include user specifications and the project plan. Comparisons are made between actual performance and the plan during operations (**assessment**). Major project control elements include projected completion date and total estimated project cost. When severe variances are experienced, the adoption of **corrective action** needs to be considered.

Control Process

Performance Standards
   Assessment
   Corrective Action

There are many tools to control project development. We review three representatives here, in the area of personnel management, accounting, and work authorization.

Responsibility Assignment

A project team is formed to bring people with a variety of skills together to accomplish the project's objectives. A project responsibility chart is a simple device commonly used to clearly state who is responsible for each project activity (Figure 6.1).

Activities: Develop Project Plan	User	PM	CE	SA	PT
A1 Initial project plan	A	I		X	
A2 Detailed plan of system modules				X	C
A3 Revise overall project plan	d	d			
A4 Complete resource, time, and cost estimates			P	X	C
A5 Review	d	d	C	C	C
A6 Final plan revision	I	I		X	I

Personnel:	Responsibility:
User who the system is to be built for	X – executes task
PM project manager	D – solely responsible for decision
CE cost estimator	d – shared decision responsibility
SA systems analyst	P – manages work - controls progress
PT production team	C – needs to be consulted
	I – needs to be informed
	A – available for advice

Figure 6.1 Example of a responsibility chart

Note that the RACI (Responsible, Accountable, Consulted, Informed) charts discussed in Chapter 6 are closely related to the responsibility chart given in Figure 8.1. Both forms can be used to clearly delineate the responsibilities of all parties involved. Also valuable is the information related to who must be consulted, informed, or is available for advice.

Budget

The traditional means of implementing cost control is **variance analysis**. Accurate measurement requires accurate identification of the quantities of work involved. Some costs are nonlinear, making it more difficult to estimate costs. This is especially true in information system projects, where progress is uncertain until testing is complete.

Cost control works most effectively when it is tied to work packages. **Work packages** include work descriptions, time-phased budgets, work plans and schedules, resource requirements, and assignments of responsibility. To make sense of cost reports, managers need to keep up with changes, generated by schedule delay, differences in planned and actual times, and changes in the scope of work. The **earned value concept** is very useful to project management in this process. Earned value is the measure of the budgeted value of work that has been accomplished. Earned value indicates how much of the budget was planned to have been spent in order to do the amount of work done so far. This concept operates on the **standard time unit**, which measures work accomplished in terms of what a normal, prudent worker with average luck would accomplish in that time unit. Standard hours are traditionally used in manufacturing. Other time units, such as day or week, can be used as well. A standard week is probably more appropriate for information systems work. This can be useful in measuring the efficiency of a work unit. It also focuses on activity completion. Calculations are shown in Table 6.1.

Table 6.1 Earned value calculations

Work package	Budgeted	% Complete	Earned value	Actual
A	20	100	20	25
B	10	100	10	8
C	12	50	6	6
D	20	75	15	15
Totals			51	54

In this example, work packages A and B are completed, so the earned value is easy to calculate. The measures for unfinished activities are more problematic, because it is difficult to accurately estimate the percentage of work completed. We have seen that in information systems projects, the final testing and debugging phases can include a great deal of unanticipated work. However, estimates of earned values can be calculated. In this case, credit is taken for half of the effort required on activity C and 75 percent of the effort required on activity D.

Relative efficiency can be calculated by dividing earned hours by actual hours. For instance, if the actual effort expended on work package A was 25, it would have been rated as 20/25 = 0.80 efficient. If work package B took 8 units of effort, the efficiency rating would be 10/8 = 1.25, or 25 percent more efficient than expected. If activities C and D had actual expenditures equal to their earned value, the efficiency of this project component as a whole would be the total earned value (51) divided by total expended effort (54) = 51/54 = 0.94, or 94 percent of planned, on average. However, these measures need to be considered in light of conditions beyond the control of the project team. If late deliveries of materials or software cause work package A to run over its budget, the inefficiency could not, in all fairness, be attributed to poor performance on the part of those responsible for doing the work of work package A. Project management needs to coordinate closely with the project team to understand the reasons for work lagging in time or running over in cost.

A more complete example with updates over time is presented. Table 6.2 gives a list of five project activities, with predecessor relationships, durations, and budget.

Table 6.2 Demonstration Input

Label	Activity	Predecessor	Duration (weeks)	Budget (K)
A	System design	None	3	50K
B	Code	A	5	150K
C	Develop interfaces	A	4	80K
D	Train	C	2	30K
E	Implement	B,D	1	40K

The schedule for this project has the following early start schedule given in Table 6.3:

Table 6.3 Early start schedule

Activity	ES	EF
System design	0	Week 3
Code	Week 3	Week 8
Develop interfaces	Week 3	Week 7
Train	Week 7	Week 9
Implement	Week 9	Week 10

Assume that 5 weeks into the project, status is as given in Table 6.4:

Table 6.4 Status 5 weeks in

Activity	Full budget	Complete	Earned	Actual
System design	50	100%	50	60
Code	150	40%	60	50
Develop interfaces	80	50%	40	50
Train	30	0%	0	0
Implement	40	0%	0	0
Efficiency	150/160	=0.9375	150	160

In Table 6.4, Actual is input obtained from accounting. Completion percentages are obtained from field personnel. Earned for each activity is Full budget times percent complete. The Earned and Actual for the project are simply the sum of those elements over all activities. Efficiency is Earned over Actual (and can be calculated not only for the full project, but also for each activity). System design is only 83 percent efficient, and Develop interfaces 80 percent. These activities are having problems. Conversely, Code seems to be doing very well, at 120 percent efficiency. Overall, the project is over budget by $10K, with an efficiency of 93.75 percent.

Progress is usually monitored at least weekly, but we will demonstrate with longer intervals. Table 6.5 gives project status 10 weeks in:

Table 6.5 Status 10 weeks in

Activity	Full budget	Complete	Earned	Actual
System design	50	100%	50	60
Code	150	100%	150	160
Develop interfaces	80	100%	80	80
Train	30	67%	20	30
Implement	40	0%	0	0
Efficiency	300/330	=0.9090	300	330

In this case, efficiency slipped a bit. System design was completed at the 5- week stage, and so is the same. Code slipped, with efficiency now dropping to 93.75 percent. Develop interfaces caught up and finished at 100 percent efficiency. Train is running 10K over budget at this stage, two-thirds complete. The project efficiency overall dropped to 90.9 percent.

Table 6.6 gives data as of project completion. Subsequent to week 10, Train stayed 10K over budget. Efficiency for this activity rose because the numerator and denominator rose by the same amount. Implement came in 10K under budget, giving it the only efficiency in the positive range. The project efficiency overall rose to 94.59 percent.

Table 6.6 Completed project calculations

Activity	Full budget	Complete	Earned	Actual	Activity efficiency
System design	50	100%	50	60	0.8333
Code	150	100%	150	160	0.9375
Develop interfaces	80	100%	80	80	1.0000
Train	30	100%	30	40	0.7500
Implement	40	100%	40	30	1.3333
Efficiency			350	370	0.9459

The point is that monitoring efficiency over time helps project control by identifying where problems are occurring. Management needs to find out why and seek to rectify negative situations. Project efficiencies also can be used for evaluation of project management personnel.

People have a tendency to do the easiest work first, especially if it is important to appear as if they are making progress. In project environments, this often leads to higher levels of progress reported than is actually the case. Projects are almost always reported to be on schedule until they are about 90 or 95 percent complete. Some activities actually finish as scheduled. But many activities start to lag behind the planned completion date in the latter stages of their work. One reason for this in information systems projects is that problems are often not identified until the testing stage. Progress reports in projects should be considered suspect until actual completion. That is the principal point of the milestone concept.

A primary role of the project information system is to monitor project progress. Data is collected from a variety of sources, including materials invoices, time cards, change notices, test results, and attitude surveys. Reports convey this information to key managers. All levels of management need to be provided with the detailed information they need to identify problems and take corrective action. These reports need to identify variances. They also need to be published in a timely fashion.

Work Authorization

Authorization is a primary means of controlling projects. Upper management authorizes the project manager to proceed. The project manager in turn authorizes departments within the project management team to accomplish various elements of work through work orders. The authorization chain works its way down through the organization. Ensuring that expenditure and work activity do not proceed without authorization is a primary means of maintaining control over the project.

The data collection process works pretty much in reverse of the authorization flow. Work sections report their progress to their managers, who report up the hierarchy until, ultimately, the project manager receives summary reports. These summary reports need to focus on problems and to identify accomplishments to date and current cost performance. The project manager needs to keep upper management informed. Upper management usually uses project information to merely keep informed of activities, unless things get so bad that canceling the project appears appropriate.

Because of the uncertain nature of information systems projects, change is to be expected. Management control through work authorization is a way to manage this change. Reasons for change include:

- Change in project scope and specification
- Changes in design
- Changes to improve rate of return
- Changes to adopt improvements

The owner may desire change in project scope and specification owing to new circumstances. These can arise because of new regulations or changes in the market. Changes in design can occur if it is clear that the original plan will not work or, possibly, if new technology may now be available that is clearly better than what was known when the project was adopted. These can arise because of errors, omissions, afterthoughts, or revised needs. Such changes can offer opportunities for improvement but may also open up opportunities for major foul-ups. Changes to improve the rate of return are a financial factor, where the owner has better things to do with the money required by the project.

Changes are troublesome for project teams. The more the project is completed, the more difficult it is to adopt changes. Changes can impact project scope, cost, and time, which in turn can lead to major sources of conflict. A change review process is a very good way to consider changes as rationally as possible. Changes should be avoided unless there are compelling reasons.

Project termination may be appropriate under a variety of circumstances. Sometimes, the owner may determine that it is better to stop than to continue. This can be due to changes in the market, cost overruns, or depleted resources. When termination before completion occurs, there are a number of things that still need to be done. Final closeout activities need to be accomplished to ensure that the owner receives whatever he or she is entitled to and the project team gets their appropriate payment. There is also a need to coordinate with functional managers of the organization to return those individuals assigned to the project on a temporary basis. Other members of the project team may need to be reassigned, possibly to other projects.

Project Evaluation

Project evaluation is concerned with monitoring progress on a project. The ultimate output of project evaluation is the decision to continue with the project or to quit. There also is a need for after-action reports, providing a means to learn from the experiences of a project.

Formative evaluations refer to those that are used to control the project. Because projects involve so many interrelated activities, and are undertaken with limited resources, there can be a lot of apparent reasons why a particular activity or work package is not going well. Furthermore, it is very easy for management to think there is a problem when there really isn't.

Meetings are very important in project control. Regular meetings in such an environment are well worth the time taken. There is a need within projects to maintain high levels of communication and coordination. Regularity leads to more thorough preparation on the part of participants. Two commonly used types of meetings used to manage projects are to coordinate activities (usually fairly unstructured) and to reach decisions (usually more structured).

After-action evaluations involve first classifying completed projects into categories of success and failure. Management needs to understand why successful projects worked as well as they did. The reason could be especially favorable external conditions or, possibly, especially effective implementation by the project team. The key to success is to understand what is true for a given project.

It is also important for organizations that are continuously involved in projects of a given type to gather information about time and cost performance for specific work packages. These work packages should be measured in terms that occur across projects so that the organization obtains knowledge about what doing a particular bit of work takes. This gives the organization a tremendous advantage over time relative to their competitors who either lack their experience or fail to keep similar records.

Summary

Project control is a means to guide project efforts toward achievement of project goals. A primary means of control is to compare actual work with planned accomplishments. This requires accurate data collection and efficient dissemination of project reports.

There are many reasons that projects fail. Consideration of the failures of others is needed to increase the probability of success of a specific project. High levels of uncertainty and change require flexible project management. Experience and preparation help increase the odds of project success.

Project risk management needs to be applied throughout the life cycle of the project. Consideration of risk was important when the project was initially considered for adoption and was implemented by estimating what could go wrong in developing the project. In the organization stages of the project, there are a number of things project management can do to ensure good people are obtained, that estimates are realistic, that contingency options are available should problems arise, and that project components delivered by those outside the project organization are received in a timely fashion and perform to specifications. During the building of the project, original time and cost budgets need to be compared with actual performance to determine whether problems are arising. It is important not only to understand that problems exist, but to plan for ways of dealing with the problems that are identified.

Project control should clearly identify responsibilities for work packages and use these work packages as the basis for cost accounting. The authorization process ensures that management retains control over the project. There is a need to constantly update projected performances in order that top management has a complete picture and is capable of making decisions to continue the project based on sound, objective information.

Project evaluation provides organizations that deal with a continuous stream of projects the ability to develop a database of knowledge by work package. This gives such organizations a tremendous edge over competitors that are unable to do the same. Furthermore, careful analysis of postaction success or failure enables organizations to better understand their work environment.

PMBOK Items Relating to Chapter 6

Monitoring and Controlling Process Group—those processes required to track, review, and orchestrate the progress and performance of the project; identify any changes required; and initiate corresponding changes.

Closing Process Group—those processes performed to conclude all activities to formally complete the project.

4.4 Monitor and Control Project Work—the process of tracking, reviewing, and reporting project progress against the performance objectives defined in the project management plan.

4.5 Perform Integrated Change Control—the process of reviewing all change requests; approving changes and managing changes to deliverables, organizational process assets, project documents, and the project management plan; and communicating their disposition.

4.6 Close Project or Phase—the process of finalizing all activities across all of the project management process groups to formally complete the phase or project.

5.6 Control Scope—process of monitoring the status of the project and product scope and managing changes to the scope baseline.

6.7 Control Schedule—process of monitoring the status of project activities to update project progress and manage changes to the schedule baseline to achieve the plan.

7.4 Control Costs—process of monitoring the status of the project to update the project costs and managing changes to the cost baseline.

8.3 Control Quality—process of monitoring and recording results of executing the quality activities to assess performance and recommend necessary changes.

10.3 Control Communications—process of monitoring and controlling communications throughout the entire project life cycle to ensure the information needs of the project stakeholders are met.

11.6 Control Risks—process of implementing risk response plans, tracking identified risks, monitoring residual risks, identifying new risks, and evaluating risk process effectiveness throughout the project.

12.3 Control Procurements—process of managing procurement relationships, monitoring contract performance, and making changes and corrections as appropriate.

Thought questions

1. What is a RACI chart, and how can it aid project control?
2. Earned value calls for cooperation between engineers and accounting—how can each of these functions contribute to project control?
3. Project efficiency could be measured in terms of duration or in terms of monetary units (dollars?). What are the relative advantages and weaknesses of either?

CHAPTER 7

Microsoft Project

Key points:
- A brief introduction to Microsoft Project, intended to get novice users started
- Demonstration of key Microsoft Project elements

The past few decades have seen the development of many excellent project management software products. Microsoft Project is easy to use and is widely available. It provides excellent quantitative support in the form of critical path method (CPM), develops network graphs automatically, and has very good report generating facilities. It also has resource usage and cost accounting capabilities. The manager can use Microsoft Project to do sophisticated analysis of alternatives through resource leveling.

This chapter is meant to provide a brief introductory guide to Microsoft Project. There will be many new versions of Microsoft Project, as well as many other good new competing products. The general procedure of Microsoft Project is fairly similar for all versions.

The latest version at the time of printing was *Microsoft Project 2016*.

Demonstration Model

Assume a waterfall information system project with three jobs to schedule, including work for the following crews. You have one crew for each activity type. Estimated durations are provided for four types of activity in Table 7.1. Each job consists of:

Each activity has one crew, shared by all three projects. These crews can work on only one project at a time and need to stay with that project until their task is completed.

Table 7.1 Demonstration project durations

	Analysis (SAD)	Coding (code)	Testing (test)	Installation (install)
Project 1	3 weeks	5 weeks	3 weeks	2 weeks
Project 2	4 weeks	6 weeks	4 weeks	2 weeks
Project 3	3 weeks	4 weeks	3 weeks	2 weeks

Getting Started

The first step is to set up the project time frame. The project start date can be entered by clicking on the **Project** menu and then clicking on **Project Information** (Figure 7.1). There is a box for the start date and for the finish date if there is a deadline. The standard base calendar works Monday through Friday, 8:00 a.m. to 5:00 p.m. (eight working hours) and uses early start scheduling. These settings can be changed.

Working days can be specified through the project calendar. On the **Project** ribbon, click on **Change Working Time**. You are presented one monthly calendar. Other months can be accessed by the down arrow or

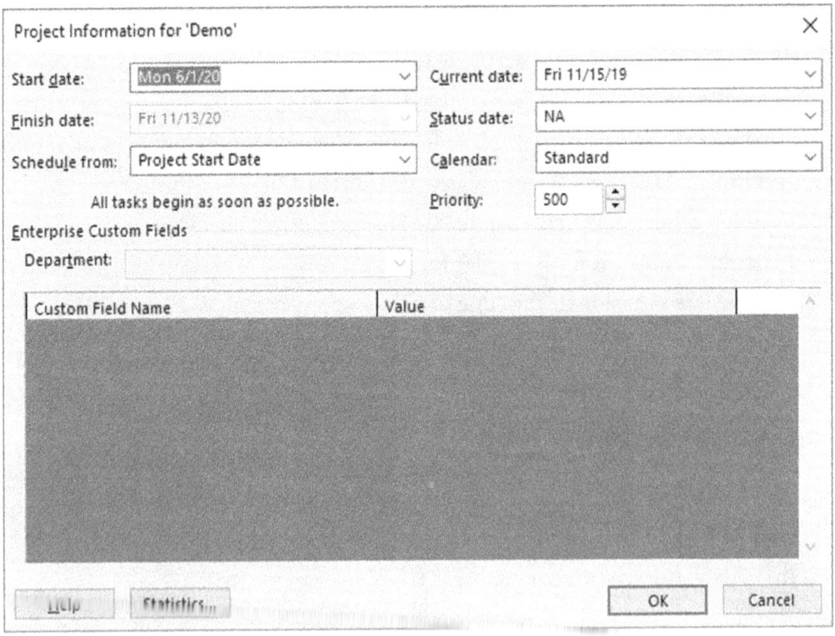

Figure 7.1 Project information screenshot

up arrow. For any particular day you wish to declare a holiday, you click on the day, and are given a window including a radio button for **non-working time**.

Project information can be entered and manipulated. There are two types of views: task views and resource views. Task information can be entered, changed, or displayed in a number of ways. The default is to set the current date as the project start date as well as the start date of the first task.

Tasks

The **Gantt Chart** view gives the Task Form on the left, with a list of project tasks with room for durations and time units, predecessor activities, and a bar chart (Figure 7.2). Tasks can be entered by row, entering the name and duration for each task in the appropriate column. Tasks can be inserted or deleted using the **Edit** menu. There are columns for start time, finish time, and predecessors (which may be hidden and can be uncovered by sliding the Task Form to the right). Duration unit syntax is the number followed by the time unit. The abbreviations are:

m	minutes
h	hours
d	days
w	weeks

To enter a duration of 6 weeks, the entry would be **6w**. Elapsed time units can be entered to disregard weekends and other nonworking periods. If you need to schedule a task over a continuous period of time that includes nonworking time, an elapsed duration can be used. If a task is to take ten calendar days, beginning on Monday and ending on the following Wednesday, the elapsed time would be 10 elapsed days. Elapsed durations are entered by preceding the time units with the letter **e**. For instance, if a task is to take ten calendar days, the entry for duration would be **10ed**.

For our demonstration project, we can set a project start date of June 1, 2020. Initial data is entered in Task Name for activities, with

Task Mode	Task Name	Dur	Start	Finish	Pr	Resrc Name	Total Slac...
	SAD Project 1	3 wks	Mon 6/1/20	Fri 6/19/20		SAD	3 wks
	Code Project 1	5 wks	Mon 6/22/20	Fri 7/24/20	1	Code	3 wks
	Test Project 1	3 wks	Mon 7/27/20	Fri 8/14/20	2	Test	3 wks
	Install Project 1	2 wks	Mon 8/17/20	Fri 8/28/20	3	Install	3 wks
	SAD Project 2	4 wks	Mon 6/1/20	Fri 6/26/20		SAD	0 wks
	Code Project 2	6 wks	Mon 6/29/20	Fri 8/7/20	5	Code	0 wks
	Test Project 2	4 wks	Mon 8/10/20	Fri 9/4/20	6	Test	0 wks
	Install Project 2	2 wks	Mon 9/7/20	Fri 9/18/20	7	Install	0 wks
	SAD Project 3	3 wks	Mon 6/1/20	Fri 6/19/20		SAD	4 wks
	Code Project 3	4 wks	Mon 6/22/20	Fri 7/17/20	9	Code	4 wks
	Test Project 3	3 wks	Mon 7/20/20	Fri 8/7/20	10	Test	4 wks
	Install Project 3	2 wks	Mon 8/10/20	Fri 8/21/20	11	Install	4 wks

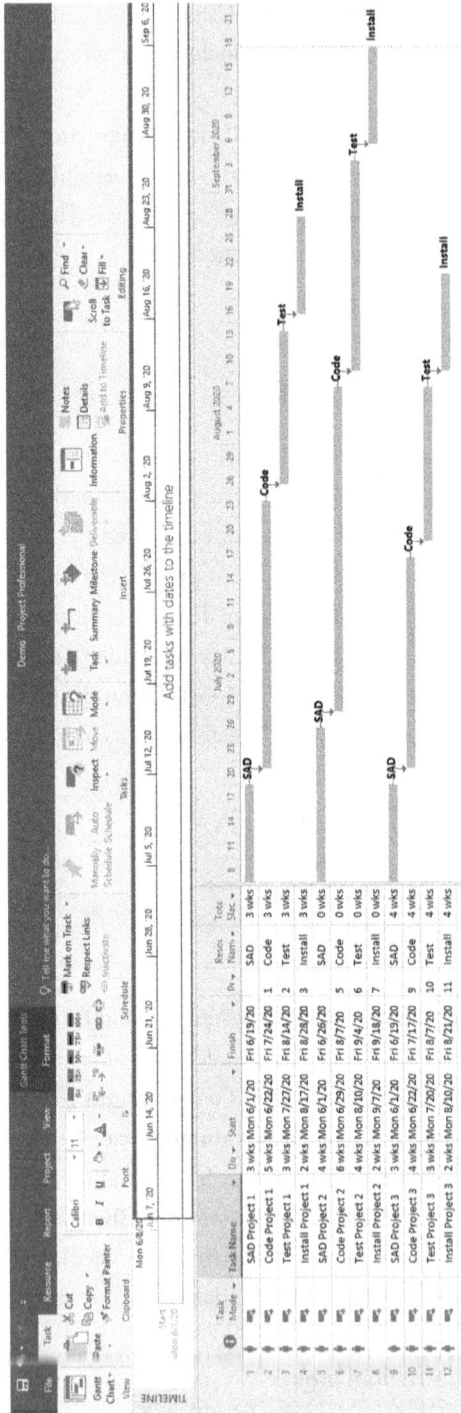

Figure 7.2 Gantt Chart view

Durations and Predecessors, as in Table 7.1, and resources by activity. We will change the default Task Mode from Manual to Automatic to allow Microsoft Project to update durations as we add progress to date and to adjust the schedule when leveling resources. The initial schedule prior to leveling resources is shown in Figure 7.2:

Note that overbooked resources are indicated in the left column with the red outline of a human.

The approach used above is fixed duration. Fixed duration is obtained by selecting the Fixed check box on the Task Form or typing yes in the Fixed Field of a task table. Task durations can be based on the amount of work required and the number of resource units assigned to it if resource-driven scheduling is used. If this is not done, when multiple resources are assigned to a task, Microsoft Project will divide the entered duration by the number of resources assigned. This is appropriate in many other environments but generally not in information systems projects. Therefore, resource-driven scheduling should be turned off. This may require clicking on each task on the Gantt Chart view and clearing the "Effort Driven" box for each task.

Predecessor relationships (along with durations) are all that there is to the critical path model. The conventional predecessor relationship is finish to start (a following activity cannot start until all predecessors are complete). In reality, other relationships might be appropriate, such as start-to-start (SS), where a following activity can start as soon as its predecessor begins; finish-to-finish (FF), where a following activity cannot finish until its predecessor finishes; or start-to-finish (SF), where a following activity cannot finish until its predecessor starts. All of these relationships can be used in Microsoft Project. In the Predecessor column, list the number of all predecessor activities. If activity 1 is a predecessor to activity 2, for activity 2 the predecessor is 1. The default is finish to start, and this does not have to be specified. For any of the other three relationships, specification is entered using the two-letter qualifier. For instance, if there is an FF relationship, the predecessor for activity 2 would be 1FF.

Sometimes, following activities can start before the predecessor activity is completed. For instance, if activity 2 can start after 5 days of activity 1 is completed, the predecessor relationship for activity 2 would be 1SS+5d. There is also a Lag column that can be used on the Task

Information window that can be accessed by double clicking on the activity and selecting the Predecessors tab.

Tasks can also be entered on the Task Form, or the Task Sheet. The **critical path** is the set of activities on a connected path that must be completed as estimated, or the project completion will be delayed. The critical path can be identified in many ways, the most direct of which is to click on the Format tab, and then on the **Critical Tasks** box. The Gantt Chart will now display critical tasks in a distinctive color or bar code as in Figure 7.3:

The critical path here is the set of four activities for Project 2, because it is the longest path. CPM assumes unlimited resources, which we know to be not true. We will level for resources a bit later.

There are many views available. The Network Diagram view gives Figure 7.4:

If you have milestones (activities indicating closure for a block of activities—defined as having zero duration), they would be indicated with a double block. This view gives the best graphical description of predecessor relationships. Within each box, the task identification number, duration, start time, and finish time are reported.

The **Task Sheet** is a spreadsheet format. It can be used to quickly create a list of tasks and information and to assign resources. It also can be used to review progress by comparing planned and actual progress. You can enter task start dates and finish dates directly if you want, but these will lock that activity into the given time frame. Usually, project management intent is best met by letting the software calculate the start dates and finish dates from the duration and predecessor input. Figure 7.5 gives a Task Sheet, with overbooked resources indicated with a red figure in the left column.

The **Task Form** allows you to enter task name with duration, one task at a time. The Task Form is displayed to the left of the Gantt Chart on the prior page. There are boxes to enter the task information, including the percentage complete. Resources required can also be entered on the Task Form.

Calendar

The **Calendar** view gives a monthly calendar showing tasks and durations. This view can be used to show the tasks scheduled in a specific period. The Calendar view (Figure 7.6) is obtained from the **View** menu.

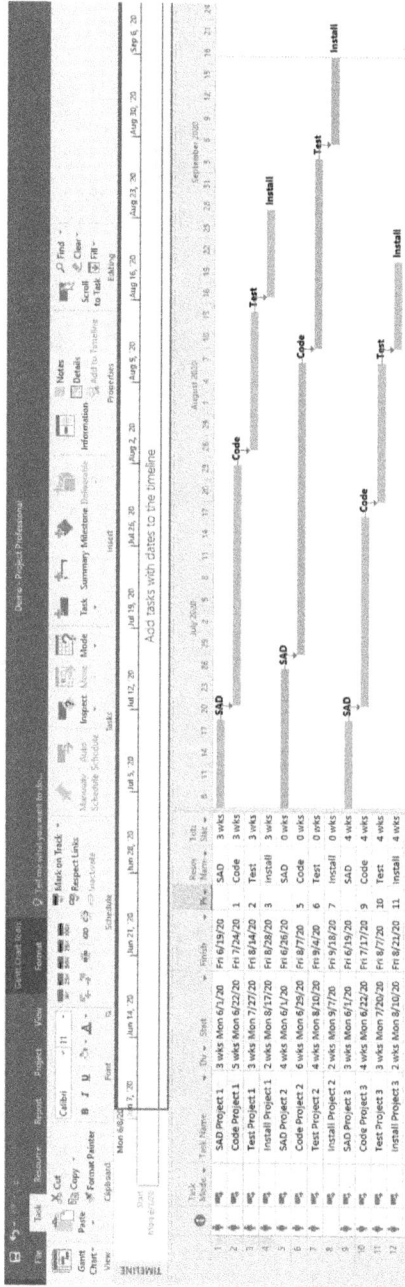

Figure 7.3 Gantt Chart view with critical path

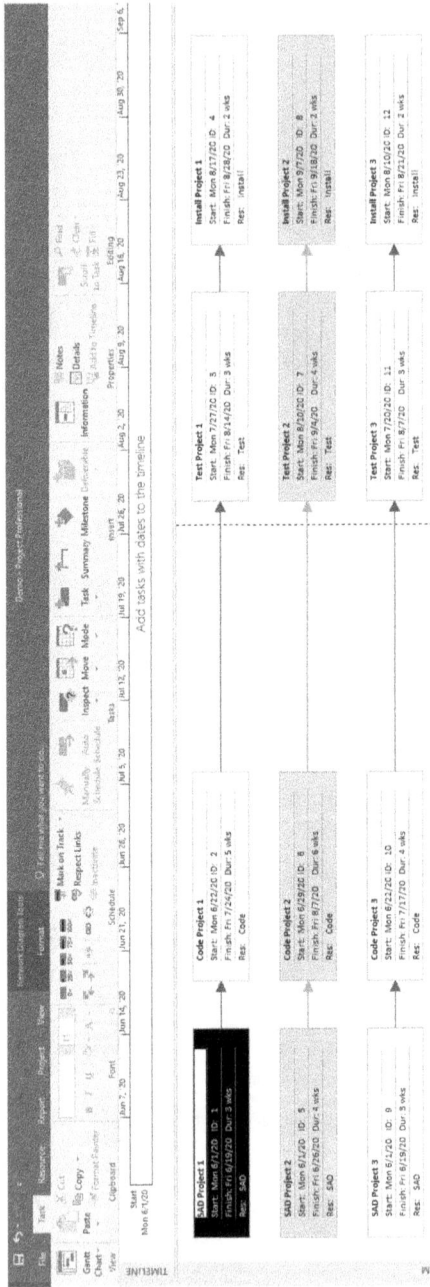

Figure 7.4 Network chart

	Task Mode	Task Name	Du	Start	Finish	Pr	Reso Name	Tot Slac
1		SAD Project 1	3 wks	Mon 6/1/20	Fri 6/19/20		SAD	3 wks
2		Code Project 1	5 wks	Mon 6/22/20	Fri 7/24/20	1	Code	3 wks
3		Test Project 1	3 wks	Mon 7/27/20	Fri 8/14/20	2	Test	3 wks
4		Install Project 1	2 wks	Mon 8/17/20	Fri 8/28/20	3	Install	3 wks
5		SAD Project 2	4 wks	Mon 6/1/20	Fri 6/26/20		SAD	0 wks
6		Code Project 2	6 wks	Mon 6/29/20	Fri 8/7/20	5	Code	0 wks
7		Test Project 2	4 wks	Mon 8/10/20	Fri 9/4/20	6	Test	0 wks
8		Install Project 2	2 wks	Mon 9/7/20	Fri 9/18/20	7	Install	0 wks
9		SAD Project 3	3 wks	Mon 6/1/20	Fri 6/19/20		SAD	4 wks
10		Code Projecr 3	4 wks	Mon 6/22/20	Fri 7/17/20	9	Code	4 wks
11		Test Project 3	3 wks	Mon 7/20/20	Fri 8/7/20	10	Test	4 wks
12		Install Project 3	2 wks	Mon 8/10/20	Fri 8/21/20	11	Install	4 wks

Figure 7.5 Task sheet for demonstration project

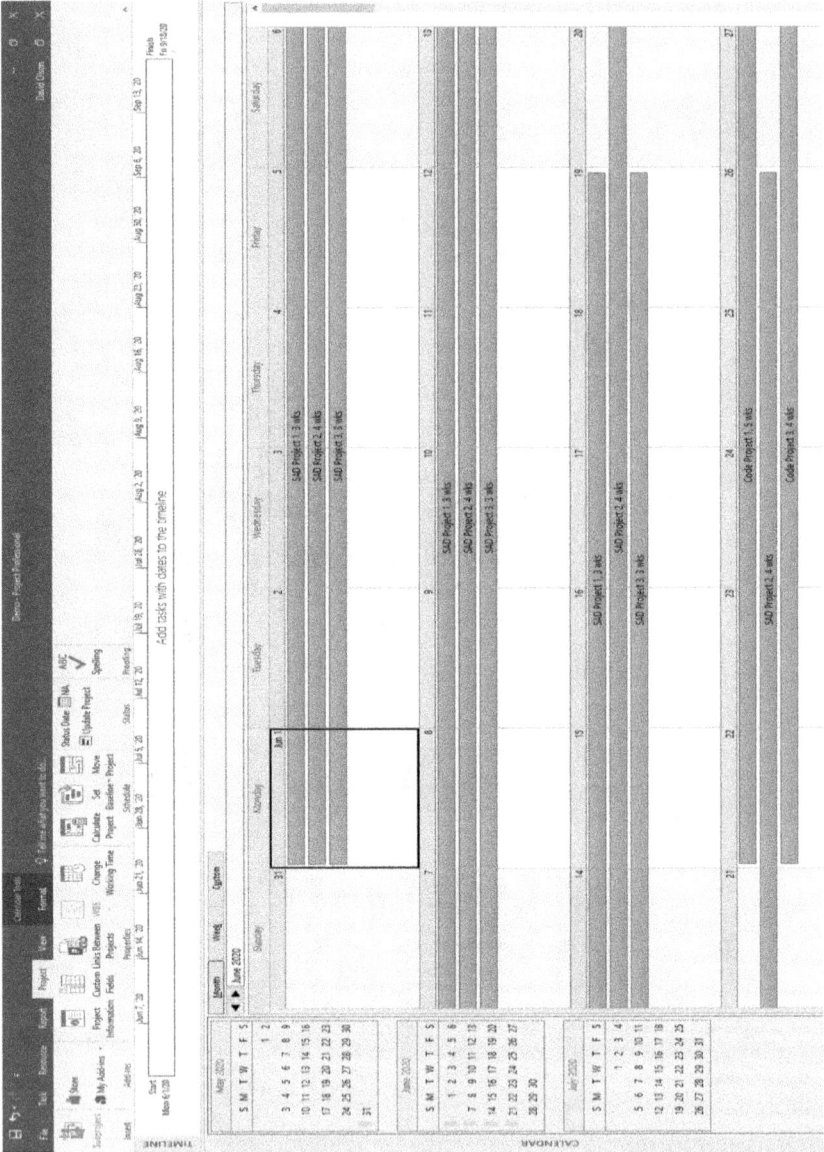

Figure 7.6 Calendar view

The calendar can be used to review tasks scheduled on particular time periods, to enter tasks and durations, and to assign resources. Unfinished activities are shown on weekends in this view, but work is not accomplished on those days.

On the Calendar view, there is an icon on the command ribbon for Change Working Time (Figure 7.7):

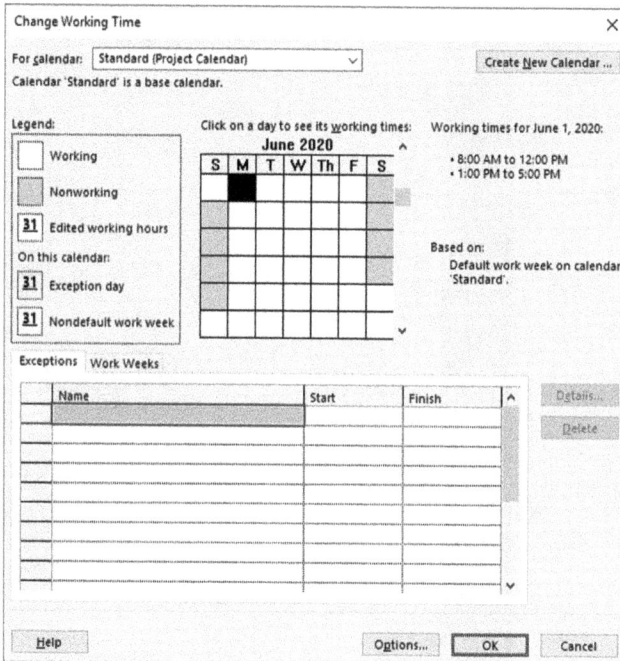

Figure 7.7 Change working time screenshot

Click on the specific day in question, and days can be made working or nonworking by clicking the appropriate radio button.

Resources

The **Resource Sheet** shows data about each resource in the project in a spreadsheet view. Resources can be entered, modified, or sorted (Figure 7.8). Cost, usage, and work information can be entered. Insert and Delete commands can be selected from the Edit menu. The Resource Sheet includes columns for full resource name, initials, a group to assign the resource to, the maximum units for each resource, and standard and overtime cost rates.

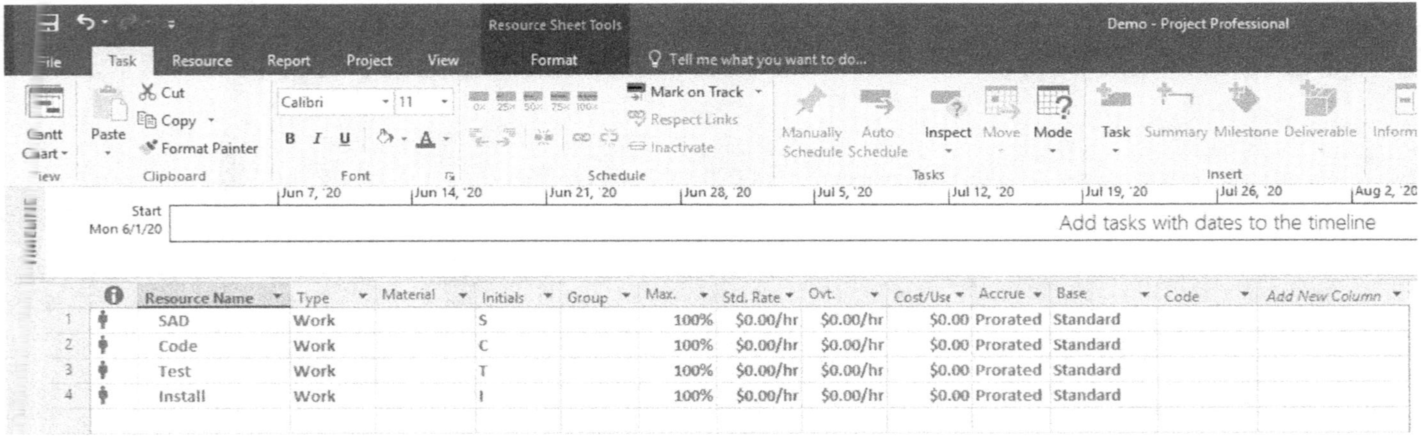

Figure 7.8 Resource sheet

If overtime rates were paid, the rate can be entered in the Ovt. Rate column. (I would recommend not using Microsoft Project for cost analysis—Excel is easier to control.)

Resources may be assigned by Microsoft Project in an effort-driven mode. This means that if you have multiple resources assigned to an activity, Microsoft Project will take the liberty of dividing the duration you entered by the number of resources. You can turn off effort-driven scheduling from the **Tools** menu, clicking on **Options**, the **Schedule** tab, and clearing the box for "New tasks are effort driven."

The Resource Graph shows resource allocation of a particular resource by time (the report for Code resource is shown in Figure 7.9). This view shows the user which resources are overallocated, and by how much, as well as the percentage of usage capacity for those resources not overallocated.

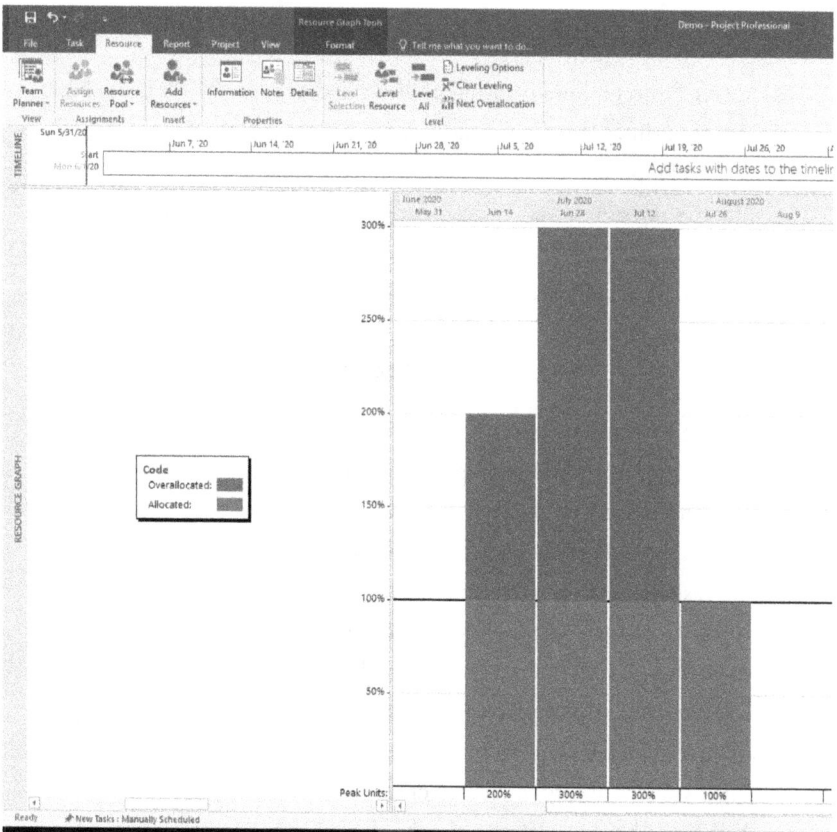

Figure 7.9 Resource graph

Overscheduled resources are shown in red on Microsoft Project. In this case, we can see that the one systems analyst available is overscheduled. In fact, we need three systems analysts in mid-January.

There is a Resource Graph for each resource. The arrow buttons at the bottom on the left scroll through these resources. The arrow buttons at the bottom on the right scroll through time. The drop-down menu on the top allows selection of a particular resource.

Resource Usage lists resources showing allocation, cost, or work information by time (Figure 7.10).

The rate at which resources are used each day is shown. In this case, overused resources can be detected in tabular form whenever over 8 hours are scheduled in a given day. In this case, resource SA is overscheduled for the first three weeks displayed.

Reports

Microsoft Project allows printing of views and of reports. There are basic reports to print. The Dashboards icon yields options for burndown (Figure 7.11), project overview, work overview, and others.

The Resources reports are available for work status and overallocation of resources. The Critical Tasks icon has reports showing details of progress on critical activities, as well as other reports.

Leveling Resources

One of the most powerful tools available in Microsoft Project is Resource Leveling. You have options to prioritize tasks and the ability to specify tasks that are not to be delayed owing to resource shortage. The standard leveling method checks predecessor relationships, slack time, dates, priority, and task constraints to select tasks to delay. You have the ability to set priorities. To change resource leveling criteria, select the **Options** menu, and **Leveling**. The Automatic option will level resources as soon as they become overallocated. If you want to bar any delay in the project completion date, the **Delay Only Within Slack** box can be checked. The **Order** box gives you the ability to change criteria.

Automatic leveling delays tasks that have not been given a constraint of **Must Start On, Must Finish On**, or **As Late As Possible**. Automatic

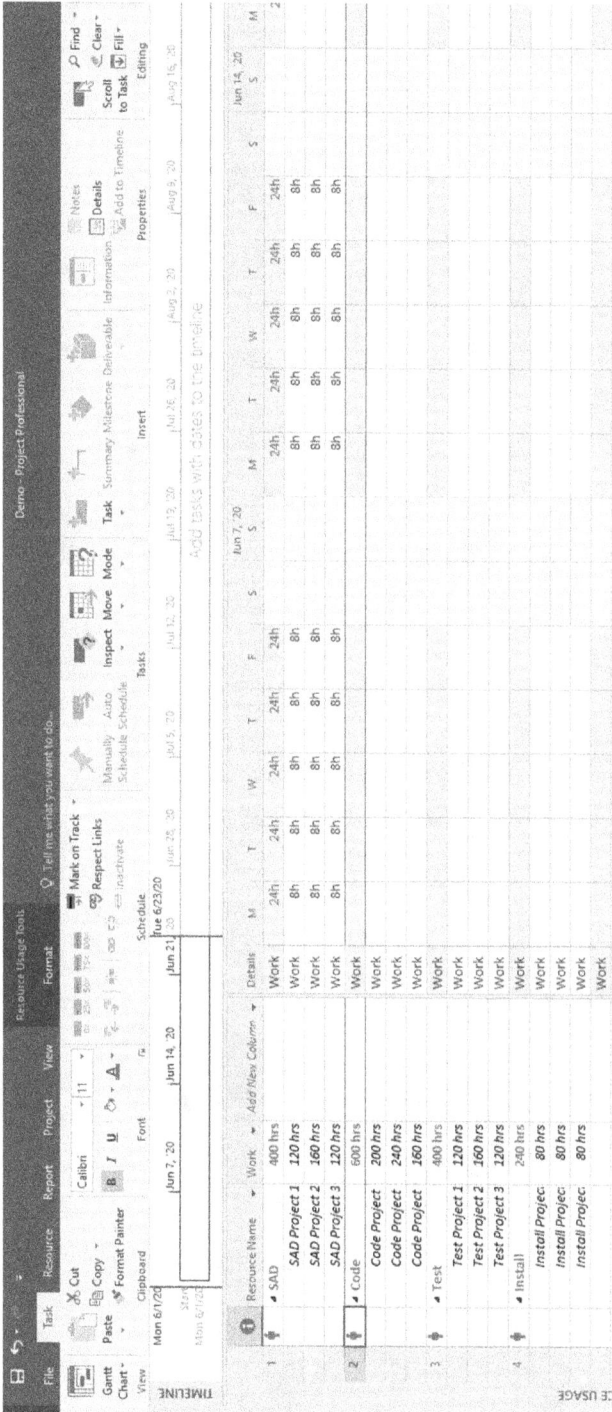

Figure 7.10 Resource usage screenshot

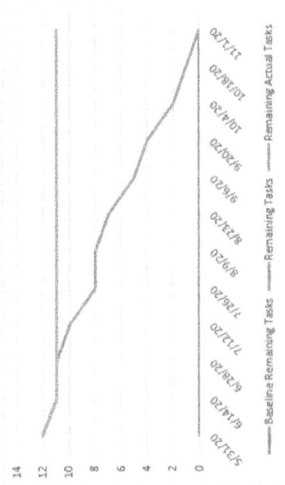

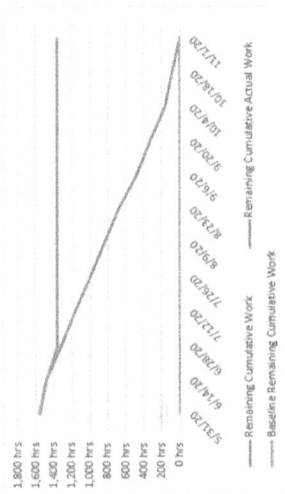

Figure 7.11 Burndown screenshot

leveling will not delay tasks if **Do Not Level** has been selected for the task. Those tasks that have been started are not delayed. Delays are assigned considering slack time, start date, priority, and task constraints.

Manual leveling can be set by selecting the Options menu, Leveling, and Manual. If this option was selected, the Level Now command can be selected from the Options menu, yielding Figure 7.12. The user can then delay activities to alleviate resource overusage. You can also resolve resource shortages by assigning overtime, or adding resources.

Updating Project Progress

Schedules can be updated on the task and resource forms. A **baseline** plan can also be saved using the **Set Plan** command from the **Options** menu. A baseline contains the original schedule, resource usage, and cost estimates. Updating a baseline plan can be accomplished on the Task Form to the left of the Gantt Chart view. Place the cursor on the task to be updated, and type Shift-F2. This gives the Task Form, where the percent complete can be entered in its box and the total revised estimated time can be entered in its box. Another way to update task usage is from the **View** bar; selecting **Task Usage**, **View** menu, **Table**, **Tracking**, drag the divider bar to the right to view the **Actual Work** field, and type the updated work value and duration as appropriate.

Work completed can be entered in the Task Form under percent Complete. The duration can be changed to reflect new circumstances. Changes in durations can be made in the duration column. The percent complete can also be set on the Gantt Chart using the mouse. From View, select Gantt Chart. Point to the left edge of a scheduled duration bar or the right edge of the progress bar. Drag the mouse until you have the percent complete you desire. You can also update using a percentage complete for each task (Figure 7.13):

We assume SAD for Project 2 is complete, SAD for Project 1 50 percent complete, and Code for Project 2 25 percent complete in Figure 7.14:

Bars are shown on the Gantt Chart to indicate work completed, which gives a good graphical view of the status of project tasks. For instance, activities 4 and 9 are running behind schedule. On the other hand, activity 10 is running ahead of schedule.

Task Name	Dur	Start	Finish	#	Reso Name	Tota Slac
SAD Project 1	3 wks	Mon 6/29/20	Fri 7/17/20		SAD	4 wks
Code Project 1	5 wks	Mon 8/10/20	Fri 9/11/20	1	Code	4 wks
Test Project 1	3 wks	Mon 9/14/20	Fri 10/2/20	2	Test	4 wks
Install Project 1	2 wks	Mon 10/5/20	Fri 10/16/20	3	Install	4 wks
SAD Project 2	4 wks	Mon 6/1/20	Fri 6/26/20	4	SAD	8 wks
Code Project 2	6 wks	Mon 6/29/20	Fri 8/7/20	5	Code	8 wks
Test Project 2	4 wks	Mon 8/10/20	Fri 9/4/20	6	Test	8 wks
Install Project 2	2 wks	Mon 9/7/20	Fri 9/18/20	7	Install	8 wks
SAD Project 3	3 wks	Mon 7/20/20	Fri 8/7/20	8	SAD	0 wks
Code Project 3	4 wks	Mon 9/14/20	Fri 10/9/20	9	Code	0 wks
Test Project 3	3 wks	Mon 10/12/20	Fri 10/30/20	10	Test	0 wks
Install Project 3	2 wks	Mon 11/2/20	Fri 11/13/20	11	Install	0 wks

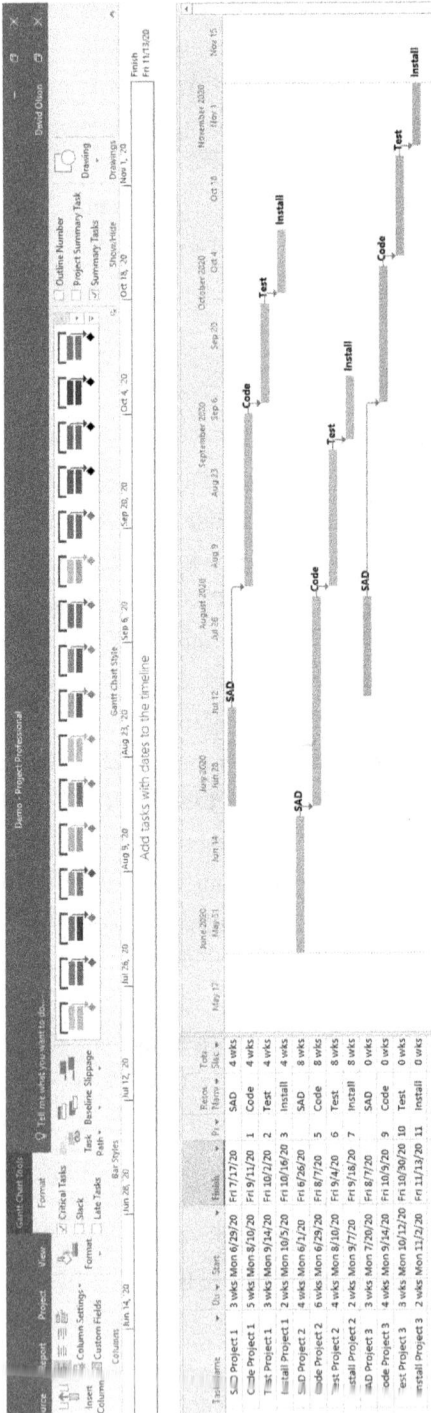

Figure 7.12 Leveled project Gantt Chart

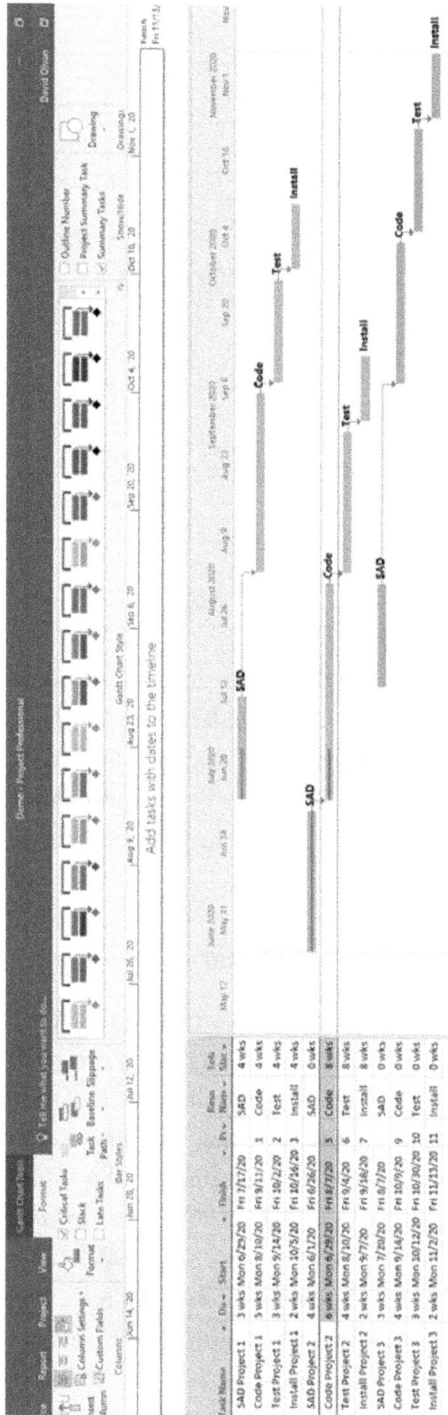

Figure 7.14 Updated Gantt Chart view

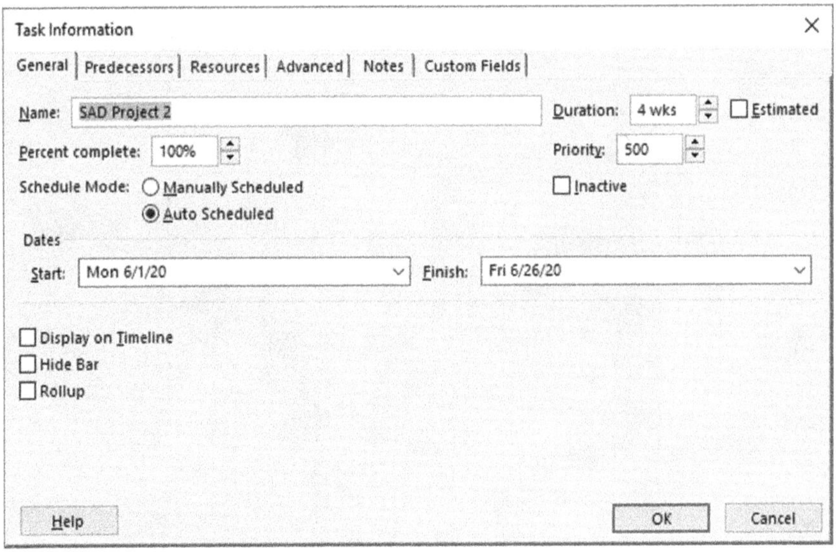

Figure 7.13 Activity updating

Milestones are points in the project that indicate the completion of a significant block of activities and provide another way to monitor project progress. Milestones can be entered in Microsoft Project as tasks with zero duration, with those tasks finishing the block as predecessors.

Different versions of the package may have different ways to enter the data.

Summary

Microsoft Project is one of many project management support systems. It is not the most sophisticated, but it is relatively easy to use and is probably the most widely used, especially by casual users of such systems. This chapter touched on some basics enabling users to get started. The Gantt Chart view is very useful for communication to others. The Network view provides another useful perspective. The Calendar view may be useful for monitoring events over time.

Microsoft Project contains quite a few useful tools. Project leveling is one of the strongest. Leveling in Microsoft Project is not optimal — it applies heuristics. But optimizing leveling is a very difficult model to solve. Leveling here gives useful means to operate. Updating is also valuable.

Overall, Microsoft Project provides a valuable communication tool for group work, which is almost definitional within projects.

Thought questions

1. What is the function of leveling? How can that be valuable in project management?
2. Microsoft Project has cost tools, but they make assumptions. Why is it safer to use Excel for cost calculations?
3. What is burndown, and how can it support project control? Is this related to fever charts?

References

Ellis, G. 2016. "Critical Chain Project Management (CCPM)." In *Project Management in Product Development: Leadership Skills and Management Techniques to Develop Great Projects.* Oxford, England: Butterworth-Heinemann.

Goldratt, E.M. 1997. *Critical Chain.* Great Barrington, MA: North River Press.

Olson, D.L. 2004. *Introduction to Information Systems Project Management.* 2nd ed. Englewood Cliffs, NJ: McGraw-Hill/Irwin.

Glossary

Chapter 1

checkpoint reviews. Meetings held at the conclusion of each project phase to determine whether the rest of the project should be completed or whether modifications to the project are required

constructive cost model (COCOMO). Software project estimation method based on a nonlinear regression against lines of code

detailed task list. Listing of work packages briefly describing work to be done

function point analysis method. Software project estimation method based on the functions the software is designed to accomplish

lines of code. Software project estimation method based on extrapolation from the estimated lines of code required

milestone. Distinct event signifying completion of a block of tasks

organization chart. Hierarchical sketch of reporting relationships among the people in an organization

planning process. Steps of information systems project management to systematically establish work activities, their schedules, budgets, and control mechanisms

RACI chart. Display of responsibility and accountability by individual, as well as identifying those who should be consulted or informed for each project activity or subactivity

responsibility matrix. Chart identifying individuals responsible for project tasks

SLOC. Simple lines of code—see Lines of Code

statement of work. Document describing what a system is to do in terms of functionality

status review meetings. Meetings to update project participants about project status, as well as to gather cost, quality, and time information

work breakdown structure. Hierarchical chart of tasks required to accomplish a project

Chapter 2

buffers. Time built into a schedule to allow for anticipated contingencies

crashing. Compressing an activity duration at a cost

critical activity. Activity with zero scheduling slack

critical path. Chain of activities with zero slack that must be completed on time for the project to meet its scheduled completion time

early start schedule. Schedule designed to accomplish each task as early as possible

feeding buffers. Buffers added to a project to protect the task in question from delays in completion of predecessor activities

float. Synonym for slack

Gantt chart. Bar chart of project tasks plotted against time units

independent slack. Slack not shared with other tasks

late start schedule. Schedule designed to accomplish each task as late as possible while maintaining expected project completion time

Network. Sketch showing the predecessor relationships among project tasks

project buffers. Buffers added to a project after its final task to ensure against delay in project completion time

resource buffers. Buffers added to a project before a task to ensure that the resources it requires are available

resource leveling. Adjusting a critical path schedule to avoid overuse of limited resources

resource smoothing. adjusting a schedule to make the use of resources more uniform, minimizing resource usage peaks and valleys

shared slack. Slack that is common to two tasks (if one of these tasks were to be late, it would exhaust its own slack, as well as the slack of the sharing task)

slack. Extra time available to accomplish a task beyond the time scheduled, while still allowing the project to be completed as scheduled

strategic resource buffers. Buffers added to projects in multiple-project environments to ensure that key resources are available for critical activities

Chapter 3

cost–time trade-off. Comparison of the time an alternative might take with its total cost impact

crashing. Comparing the impact of alternative means of accomplishing tasks

optimal. Alternative providing the greatest profit (or lowest cost if that is the objective)

Chapter 4

expected duration. Weighted average duration given estimates of minimum, most likely, and maximum

Monte Carlo simulation. Models using statistical distributions and drawing random numbers in order to obtain many outputs, enabling identification of expected system performance

PERT. Project Evaluation and Review Technique—a means to incorporate probability into critical path modeling

random number. Unbiased uniformly distributed continuous number drawn from the range 0 to 1, which can be converted to any distribution

simulation. Analysis drawing instantiations from probability distributions

standard deviation. Measure of dispersion (square root of the variance)

Chapter 5

buffer. Additional time added to a duration for additional safety relative to on-time completion

critical chain process. Application of the bottleneck concept to project scheduling

feeding (feeder) buffer. Buffer added at the end of a noncritical activity feeding into a critical activity, to ensure less interference with critical path

fever chart. Plotting relative use of project buffer, with the idea of identifying when critical stages are reached

project buffer. Buffer added at the end of the project

relay-race mentality. Scheduling noncritical activities to finish on their late start schedule (considering feeding buffers)

resource buffer. Buffer placed before critical activities using constrained resources

resource constraint. Resource scheduled for use on multiple activities in a project (or projects)

strategic resource buffer. Buffer applied before constrained resources are scheduled in multiple projects

Chapter 6

after-action evaluations. Postproject assessment to add to organizational learning

assessment. Monitoring project progress to identify problems

authorization. Control technique requiring managerial approval before resources are expended on an activity

benchmarking. Test of system with representative workload

control. Actions taken to keep project on target

corrective action. Managerial actions to redirect project effort

earned value concept. Standard accounting technique crediting progress with its budget value

formative evaluations. Evaluations of critical project elements

high change threshold. Policy to limit changes to project scope

incremental development. System development by iterative partial development followed by user testing to verify functionality

mission analysis. Evaluation of system component contribution with respect to organizational needs and objectives

performance standards. Specifications of a successful project (what the resulting system should do to be called a success)

preaward audits. Techniques to assure vendor capacity and reputation

prototyping. Testing of a system by developing a small-scale model so that it can be evaluated

reference checking. Contact existing users to verify adequacy of system performance

requirements scrubbing. Elimination of unnecessary project elements

standard time unit. Work measurement technique identifying typical competent effort needed to perform a specific task

technical analysis. Test of the ability of the system to function in appropriate environments

variance analysis. Accounting cost control focusing on differences between planned and actual performance

work packages. Division of project into groups of related activities

Chapter 7

baseline. Original schedule, used for purposes of comparison of progress

burndown. Plot of remaining cumulative work, to monitor project progress

calendar view. Display of the project in terms of a calendar

constrained resource. Resource needed by multiple activities, possibly at the same time

critical path. Link of sequential activities from beginning to end of the project that must be completed on time or else the project will be delayed (there can be multiple critical paths)

Gantt chart. Graphical plot of activity schedule over time

leveling. Delaying activity schedule to stay within allowable level of resources available

resource usage. Display of allocation of resources over time

resources. Entities (people, equipment, etc.) needed for completion of activities—of interest if they are shared over tasks

task. Activity to be scheduled

About the Author

David L. Olson is the James & H.K. Stuart Professor and Chancellor's Professor at the University of Nebraska. He has published research in over 200 refereed journal articles, primarily on multiple objective decision making, information technology, supply chain risk management, and data mining. David teaches in the management science, business analytics, and supply chain management areas. He has authored over 30 books, including *Decision Aids for Selection Problems*, and books on risk management, project management, and business analytics. David is associate editor of *Decision Support Systems*; *IEEE Transactions on Systems, Man, and Cybernetics;* and *Decision Sciences* and coeditor in chief of *International Journal of Services Sciences*. He has made hundreds of presentations at international and national conferences on research topics. He is a member of the Decision Sciences Institute, the Institute for Operations Research and Management Sciences, and the Multiple Criteria Decision Making Society. He was a Lowry Mays endowed Professor at Texas A&M University from 1999 to 2001. David was presented the Raymond E. Miles Distinguished Scholar award for 2002 and was a James C. and Rhonda Seacrest Fellow from 2005 to 2006. He was named Best Enterprise Information Systems Educator by International Federation for Information Processing (IFIP) in 2006. He is a Fellow of the Decision Sciences Institute.

Index

OTHER TITLES IN OUR PORTFOLIO AND PROJECT MANAGEMENT COLLECTION

Timothy Kloppenborg, *Editor*

- *The People Project Triangle: Balancing Delivery, Business-as-Usual, and People's Welfare* by Stuart Copeland and Andy Coaton
- *How to Fail at Change Management: A Manager's Guide to the Pitfalls of Managing Change* by James Marion and John Lewis
- *Core Concepts of Project Management* by David L. Olson
- *Projects, Programs, and Portfolios in Strategic Organizational Transformation* by James Jiang and Gary Klein
- *Capital Project Management, Volume III: Evolutionary Forces* by Robert N. McGrath
- *Capital Project Management, Volume II: Capital Project Finance* by Robert N. McGrath
- *Capital Project Management, Volume I: Capital Project Strategy* by Robert N. McGrath
- *Executing Global Projects: A Practical Guide to Applying the PMBOK Framework in the Global Environment* by James Marion and Tracey Richardson
- *Project Communication from Start to Finish: The Dynamics of Organizational Success* by Geraldine E. Hynes
- *The Lost Art of Planning Projects* by Louise Worsley and Christopher Worsley
- *Project Portfolio Management, Second Edition: A Model for Improved Decision Making* by Clive N. Enoch
- *Adaptive Project Planning* by Louise Worsley and Christopher Worsley
- *Passion, Persistence, and Patience: Key Skills for Achieving Project Success* by Alfonso Bucero
- *Leveraging Business Analysis for Project Success, Second Edition* by Vicki James
- *Project Management Essentials, Second Edition* by Kathryn N. Wells and Timothy J. Kloppenborg
- *Agile Working and the Digital Workspace: Best Practices for Designing and Implementing Productivity* by John Eary
- *Project-Based Learning: How to Approach, Report, Present, and Learn from Course-Long Projects* by Harm-Jan Steenhuis and Lawrence Rowland
- *Developing Strengths-Based Project Teams* by Martha Buelt and Connie Plowman
- *Scrum for Teams: A Guide by Practical Example* by Dion Nicolaas
- *Project Management and Leadership Challenges, Volume IV: Agility in Project Management and Collaboration* by M. Aslam Mirza

Announcing the Business Expert Press Digital Library

Concise e-books business students need for classroom and research

This book can also be purchased in an e-book collection by your library as

- *a one-time purchase,*
- *that is owned forever,*
- *allows for simultaneous readers,*
- *has no restrictions on printing, and*
- *can be downloaded as PDFs from within the library community.*

Our digital library collections are a great solution to beat the rising cost of textbooks. E-books can be loaded into their course management systems or onto students' e-book readers.
The **Business Expert Press** digital libraries are very affordable, with no obligation to buy in future years. For more information, please visit **www.businessexpertpress.com/librarians**.
To set up a trial in the United States, please email **sales@businessexpertpress.com**.

www.lightningsource.com/pod-product-compliance
Lightning Source LLC
Chambersburg PA
CBHW050501190326
41458CB00005B/1387